BRAVE

BRAVE

Women of the Bible and
Their Stories of Grief,
Mercy, Folly, Joy, Sex, and
Redemption

-
-
-
-
-
-
-

ALICE CONNOR

Broadleaf Books
Minneapolis

For Ariel and Annie and Abi and all the other brave,
untamed, wild, and fierce women in my life

I've had to learn how to separate what I have known and learned of God personally from what other people have done to me in the name of God.

—AMBER CANTORNA

What are you afraid of?
Not being enough.
Being too much.

—ANONYMOUS, FOUND ON
UNIVERSITY OF CINCINNATI'S CAMPUS

Contents

Introduction

How Could She Possibly?

Oh, hell. It's a sequel.

Don't worry, there isn't a trilogy in the works because I didn't really want to write this book. I wrote about all the women I wanted to in *Fierce*—the big names, the ones I'd been carrying around in my heart for years, waiting to share them with someone, anyone. My editor Lisa, patient to a fault, had to ask me several times before I threw up my hands and said, "I guess!" Rather like the moment when I took back my college boyfriend after our breakup and began to fall deeper in love with him every day until I couldn't bear to be parted from him (and now we've been married for over twenty years with two large children), once I said yes to Lisa, I began to love these ladies too.

They're an odd bunch: Matriarchs tossed together with mercenaries, various moms alongside prophets and victims, even an actual dude for good measure. I'm not trying to articulate precisely and once and for all what *really* happened but naming the ambiguity and imagining what might have been. This is a big part of feminist biblical interpretation: not making things up whole cloth but reading between the lines, taking educated guesses at what's being hinted at. We take this tack because so much of scripture and its interpretation since it was written is from a male perspective, concerned with culturally defined male activities and The Big Story that men are in charge of. This doesn't make it bad by any means, only incomplete. In the very beginning, God created humans in God's own image, male-and-female, the first human containing multitudes. Why would The Big Story working itself out in history use only men as actors?

There's so much more going on underneath any Bible story you'd care to name—more characters, more grime and intrigue and sex. I'm not supposed to talk about sexy things, though, because I'm a priest and this is a book about the Bible. We are meant to be serious and wholesome, the Bible and me, and there's no place for sex-having, much less sex-enjoying, in church. Only, as I talked about in *Fierce*, the Bible is, in fact, R-rated for language, violence, and sexual situations, often all at the same time. The Bible reflects back to us what we're going through, what we see daily in the news, what we fear, and what we desire. The Bible is R-rated because our lives are R-rated. It's moving and transformative precisely because it deals with the real, unsanitized version of existence.

In seminary, they told us the same thing: all this stuff we're teaching you, you can't tell your congregations; they can't handle it. Not the "God loves you" stuff; that's fine—it's the ahistorical stuff, the editing of scripture across generations, the mythic nature of all of Genesis and Exodus, the pointing out of Jesus' violent nature in the midst of his countercultural ministry, God's concern for how we spend our money and complete silence on homosexuality. That stuff won't fly, they told us. You can't.

Oh, I can, and I will.

I'll tell you what, though—after *Fierce* came out, when I was constantly posting on social media and sharing the book trailer and drumming up interest, I got a surprising number of comments from random men quoting Galatians 3:28 at me. In retrospect, maybe it wasn't that surprising. If you're not super familiar with your biblical citations, that one reads, "There is no longer Jew or Greek, there is no longer slave or free, there is no longer male and female; for all of you are one in Christ Jesus." Beautiful, right? There are connection and deep freedom found in the community of God. But that's not what these dudes were after. They meant, "You can't do that." Whether the emphasis was on *you* or *that* doesn't matter. They meant, "How could she possibly write this?" They thought Paul meant that not only was there no point in raising up women's stories in this glorious, postgender world we all know we live in, but it was their responsibility to tell me I wasn't allowed. They felt threatened, and bless them, they just didn't understand the wide-open vision God has for creation, a vision that spreads its arms beyond the limits we impose on it.

Aside from these few misguided fellas, all I've heard for years now is thousands of people who felt like a wall came down when they read these stories. Like they'd suspected there was more to what they'd learned but didn't know where to look, like they'd longed to see themselves in scripture but had never been taught, like their shoulders unhunched and their hearts cracked open just a little and their eyes got wider like a Disney princess suddenly coming across a handsome vista or a bucolic man. So you're damn right it's a sequel, and I haven't said everything there is to say.

I wanted desperately to include a chapter this time about biblical trans people. But there are no trans characters in the Hebrew and Christian Bibles. *Fierce* and *Brave* are ostensibly about women in scripture, but they're more about those excluded from power structures and cultural memory for not being men. There are some who say the eunuchs mentioned here and there could be understood as trans and, indeed, might be included in the sweeping arc of queer history, though only the Ethiopian eunuch and Esther's friend have any substantive conversation in scripture. There's a playwright who wrote Joseph (of *The Amazing Technicolor Dreamcoat*) as a trans man, and I am so here for it. Gender isn't binary, and I guarantee you there are characters in our Bible who didn't fit their culture's definitions. But we don't really know who they were.

We sing a song at the Edge House, the campus ministry I serve, that may get at what I want to say. The lyrics are "In God's image, I was created. Male and female God created me." At first glance, it seems to suggest a gender binary, but recall the second story of creation in Genesis when God created the first human, the *adam*, genderless and containing all gender. God created humans in God's own image, male-and-female: the most appropriate pronoun for God is *they*. God is male-and-female; God is plural and singular. (The singular use of the pronoun *they* goes back hundreds of years in English, and most of us use it casually every day.) As a cisgender woman, I don't have direct experience, but I try to draw connections to trans experience here and there in this book because God didn't make no trash. To my trans siblings: when I write about women living outside of conventional power or being tricksters or victims or businesspeople or just living their damn lives, those women include you in their embrace.

I use the phrase "how could she possibly" a lot in this book, mostly in the mouths of people who dismiss the experiences of women and minorities. It comes from a deep place within us, this sense of judgment and deserving and this inability to conceive of another person's humanity. But how we interact with the world is just the opposite: it's all about possibility.

I'm going to confess something to you here: I read a lot of fan fiction. You know, the further adventures of Sherlock Holmes and John Watson where also they have a lot of sex. I mean, not always—sometimes it's a tender exploration of Sherlock's asexuality or John's PTSD. Or it's a slice-of-life piece about a case referenced in the show but that the viewers didn't see. Or it's a poetic treatment of their friendship during an apocalyptic climate event where the earth stops rotating on its axis. It's a way to explore characters and worlds and even our own lives in more depth in the context and comfort of a well-loved story. Fan fiction is about possibility. I framed this as a confession, but I'm not ashamed of it at all.

When I was writing *Fierce*, I went back and forth with the aforementioned editor Lisa about the Mary Theotokos chapter because with each revision, she said, "It feels like fan fiction." We eventually came to an understanding of what she meant by that, and I fixed it and moved on, but in the moment, I kept replying,

"But Lisa, every chapter I'm writing is fan fiction." I'm taking an original piece of art that has moved me and expanding on it, exploring what it could mean, transforming it and being transformed. And funnily enough, much of scripture is a form of fan fiction as well—fans of the Matriarchs and Patriarchs writing stories about them, fans of Saint Paul writing more letters in his voice about the things they were concerned about. It doesn't make it lesser, just like something being metaphorical doesn't make it lesser: a metaphor is more than the literal meaning; it adds to it. Fan fiction is more than the literal story.

In scholarly circles, they call them *transformative works* rather than *fan fiction* because the writer is making something entirely new from the building blocks of the original. Fan fiction isn't simply porn-laden adventures of characters we love; it's about investment in something we are passionate about, it's participation in the creative process, and it's about what we're missing. Even without adding stories to the main narrative, readers of *Pride and Prejudice*, almost to a person, feel that it is their story, that there is communal ownership of the story beyond author Jane Austen. Obviously, they didn't write it, but it has taken on a life and a possibility beyond the words on the page. Every movie or television adaptation is scrutinized for what they kept, left out, or added; every actor considered reverently against the book; every glance or touch holding an entire novel's meaning that they then write, either in their hearts or on paper. Neil Gaiman has made his professional name writing fan fiction, by his own admission. Fans of Cervantes' *Don Quixote* wrote sequels within his lifetime, so he wrote a second book to set the record straight. Half of the letters attributed to Saint Paul in the Christian Testament were likely written by his followers in his name. The Song of Solomon probably wasn't written by Solomon, and the Psalms, while attributed to King David, were probably written by others in his name. Sometimes these transformations are orgasmic, but more often, they're cathartic.

I'm telling you all this because there's a form of biblical interpretation Jewish rabbis do called midrash, which is retelling and expanding on scriptural stories in order to understand them better. They add in motivations, additional details, and entirely new scenes. My friend Rabbi Yitzi was very clear with me that Jews do not think of midrash as fan fiction. Midrash is imaginative, but it is also authoritative, canonical even. Hagar, for example, is understood as an Egyptian princess who willingly chose servitude with Sarah and Abraham because of their faithfulness, even though this is very much not in the Genesis stories, and Yitzi and his wife Dina do not find this to be an optional detail. But I wonder if there's a fundamental misunderstanding about what fan fiction is, that it is shallow and ridiculous as opposed to compassionate and enlightening. I can tell you that the piece entitled "Alone on the Water" about Sherlock Holmes discovering that he is dying of cancer and John Watson caring for him in those last days has me weeping every single time and trying to make sense of sudden death.

When the people of Israel were ripped out of their homes and their Temple was destroyed in 586 BCE, they tried to make sense of it. They wrote songs and scholarly essays and myths and fairy tales and historical fiction to try to understand how this trauma could possibly have happened. Our ancestors were just living their lives, weren't they? They were doing the best they could, and then there was Babylon invading and pillaging, and where was God? I'll tell you where: God was right pissed off at Israel and was grieving by their side as well. This is how we got most of the Hebrew scriptures—human beings taking the ancestral stories they'd heard all their lives and revising them, transforming them, and retelling them to a new generation in an attempt to keep such tragedy from befalling anyone again.

And this is why I call what I'm doing in this book fan fiction. Because some of it is just picking up what the text is laying down and offering it to you like a crow with a shiny bit of foil. "Check this out; have you seen this?" And some of it is imagining what was going on behind the text, the meaningful looks people gave each other, the unspoken tensions, the physical connections and violence we gloss over when we read it in church. I wrote this work of fan fiction because I am constantly wrestling with scripture, demanding a blessing and walking away with a limp. I wrote it to answer the question, "How could you possibly?" I wrote it for those of you who longed for more after *Fierce*, for those who struggle to find yourselves in scripture, and for those of you who have never heard of these women and still recognize them as family. I wrote it because I couldn't possibly not. And I wrote it because I'm a fan.

God Is Not a Man

I'm Every Woman; It's All in Me

> From whose womb did the ice come forth, and who has given birth to the hoarfrost of heaven?
> —JOB 38:29

Do you think dogs have gender? I was talking about this with my friends Nat and Rachel some time ago and have been thinking about it ever since. In other words, does my girl dog Molly know she's a girl, and does that come with any other understandings about herself? Obviously, dogs have biological sex, but that's not the same as gender—a more spiritual, emotional, and ontological experience that may or may not overlap with genitals. Do dogs have a concept in their brains or interactions of being masculine or feminine? And further, do dogs have culture and thus some sort of expectations that change over time about gender and how it's expressed?

Our concepts of masculinity and femininity are grounded in the culture we live in—what makes something one or the other changes based on your era, your location, your socioeconomic status. Did you know that women in the Viking era managed the family's money and were able to divorce their husbands as needed? Did you know that the concept of pink for girls and blue for boys is a mid-twentieth-century innovation brought to us by a department store trying to sell us more stuff? Or that high-heeled shoes were developed for and worn for centuries by men before women started wearing them? Louis XIV of France was deeply enamored of how tall they made him and how sculpted they made his calves look. And a bifurcated trouser is a fairly recent innovation for men and women both—there were hose and leggings and such for centuries, but they were almost always worn with a tunic, a dress, a kilt, or another skirted garment by everyone. Which then leads me to ask you, dear reader, Do you think a dog would wear trousers on their back half (two legs) or their bottom half (four legs)?

What were we talking about? Oh, right, whether dogs have gender. And whether God has gender.

The only sex organ God has in the Bible is a uterus. Does that surprise you? It's not like God's genitals are frequently discussed anywhere, really, but in Job, God asks rhetorically, "Did I not give birth to this whole dang universe from my very own womb? I did, Job, so shut it," or words to that effect. When Jacob blesses his twelve strapping boys just before his death, he arguably calls upon the blessings of God's womb. Moses castigated the people in song, telling them they'd forgotten the God who had given birth to them. God gives birth to creation and to each of us and is also a midwife to those births. No penis or testicles to be seen. So if God has a gender related to some sort of divine biology, it must be female. But of course God doesn't have genitals, and genitals don't determine gender anyway. Gender is experience and expression and identity, not biology, even though they frequently line up in humans. Does God identify with any one gender? Given the scriptural witness and the breadth of human experience, it seems incredibly unlikely. In this essay, I will contend that *they* is the most fitting pronoun for God, but before that, I will argue that *she* is not only appropriate for God but necessary.

In the beginning—the beginning of the Bible, the beginning of the story we tell about ourselves as Jews and Christians, the beginning of all that is—the spirit of God hovered over the waters of chaos, breathing in and out across the water, making ripples, waiting, and then creating. This spirit is *ruach*, "breath," and she is feminine.

And in the beginning, participating in creating all that is, was God's Wisdom, *chokhmah* in Hebrew, *sophia* in Greek, both feminine. She was with God and she was God and through her, all things were made. Beyond grammar, beyond history, God's Wisdom is a woman who even now walks among us.

And in the beginning, God made humans, male-and-female, in God's own image. Not one or the other in God's image but both of them: they reflected God's attitude, God's care, God's investment in creation, together. Long before anyone talked of feminism or inclusive language in worship, God was moving and making, and she was doing it as a woman as well as a man. Only, again, not so much with the genitals.

When God renewed the covenant with Abram and Sarai and changed their names, God used the name *El Shaddai* for herself, which means "God of the mountains" and also, because we humans name things after our bodies, "God of the breasts."

When the prophets saw the glory of God appearing in the Temple—God's bright, shining, actual presence yet also only an aspect of the divine—the glory was called *shekinah*, and she was feminine.

Jesus himself is described as Wisdom, like *chokhmah* and *sophia*. Saint Paul directly identified Jesus of Nazareth as the Wisdom of God. Jesus the Word was in the beginning with God and was God, and through the Word, all things were made. The Word of God is a creative force, calling things into being, making things happen simply by existing.

And between and among these anchor moments in the Bible are stories of God as laboring woman, God as nursing mother, God as midwife, God as mother hen and mother bear, God as a woman desperately searching for a lost coin and kneading yeast into bread dough.

Let me give you an example from Proverbs. In chapter 8, there's a lovingly crafted song about God's Wisdom and her work at the beginning of all that is. Before God created anything else, she says, God created her. Before water and soil and seeds and stars, Wisdom hovered and waited. And then they sprang into action: God marked out the boundaries and drew the shape of things, and Wisdom built them—crafted at her bench the mountains, the sea, the clouds. God thought up the creatures and the vegetables, and Wisdom shaped them and taught them to grow. Wisdom and Creator, somehow both separate and inseparable, delighted in each other and in what they made.

Even after the Christian scriptures were officially agreed upon, the big names of theology were speaking of God in feminine terms. Julian of Norwich wrote in the late 1300s, "A mother can hold her child tenderly to her breast, but our tender mother, Jesus, can lead us in friendly fashion into his blessed breast by means of his sweet open side." Thirteenth-century Dutch mystic Hadewijch (my most favorite mystic) consistently referred to God as *Love*—both grammatically feminine and personified in her poems as a woman. And Anselm, archbishop of Canterbury, wrote in 1072, "And you, Jesus, sweet Lord, are you not also a mother? Truly, you are a mother, the mother of all mothers who tasted death in your desire to give life to your children." No less an authority than Saint Augustine wrote in the late fourth century about God in womanly terms.

You could make the case—and many have—that some of these words I'm using as "proof" that God is at least a little bit female are only grammatically feminine, not essentially so. *Chair* is feminine in French—"la chaise"—but chairs are not gendered in everyday conversation. Indeed, most languages that use gendered grammar don't generally intend gender expectations related to those designations. I am willing to grant this point (grumpy commenters on Amazon and Facebook, take note), but I am not willing to concede that God does not have a feminine essence. In the examples I shared, God shows up not just grammatically feminine but essentially feminine and sometimes physically feminine.

Women feed people, every day, in glorious ways and prosaic ways and even desperate ways. So does God. Women carry water for miles to their villages, soothing the sharp ache of thirst and washing away filth. So does God. Women tend to wounds and teach children and demand justice and make art and raise crops and protect the vulnerable, and so does God. Whatever your culture, God shows up like women show up.

A couple of years ago, I took nine college students to Spain to walk some of the Camino de Santiago, an ancient pilgrim path across Europe to the cathedral at Santiago de Compostela. Along the way, we lost three students. I know, it was hideous. Our group tended to spread out a bit on the path, the people in the front stretching their legs but then stopping periodically to wait for those of us who were slower, so not seeing someone for a while wasn't unusual. But several hours and a massive rainstorm later, we still hadn't seen them. By this time, the rest of us were at the hostel, and I was anxiously peering out the window, walking a mile up the path in the rain and asking other pilgrims if they'd seen them, wondering if they were lost forever, wringing my hands and sobbing. You might well say, "They're adults, one of them speaks Spanish, the path isn't that hard to find if you ask around," and you would be right. It turns out, they weren't lost; they'd only veered off the path and then back on again without knowing it.

When I caught sight of them coming toward the hostel, I almost collapsed in relief. I felt like the father in the story of the prodigal son—it says, "While the son was still far off, his father saw him" because he'd been squinting off into the distance every day, longing for a glimpse of his lost son. The father in that story is usually understood to be God, and I, in that moment, was that father, embodying God's desire to see my students' faces again. All of my soul was leaning toward them, toward the direction they should be coming from, and I was full to the brim with joy to see them.

My gender and the gender of the father in the story are simultaneously relevant and unimportant. How we identify ourselves, the things we've learned, and what's important to us because of our gender identities are not nothing. Gender, however we understand it for ourselves, means something, and it's long past time to include more than one in our conversations with and about God. Regardless of our genitals or internal understanding, every one of us can wait, anxiously staring at the horizon to see our child appear. Every one of us can lead troops into battle or care tenderly for someone who's hurt. And God encompasses all of our particularities and universalities, God as the father and the king and the midwife and the hen. God is a woman as much as she is a man—gender-fluid, you might say, or nonbinary.

And here we come to *they* as the most appropriate pronoun for God. It strikes me that the doctrine of the Trinity merits it—*they* includes the possibility of multiple persons and multiple genders, and *they* has been used as a singular pronoun for hundreds of years anyway. The word holds within itself both singular and plural; like God, it has a complexity that can't quite be named. God the Father who is also God Sophia becomes flesh in the Gospel of John—at that point, God is clearly gendered male, and yet this brief thirty-three human years is a blip in God's long, ungendered existence.

So why do we constantly see imagery of God as a man, typically old, white, and weirdly fit? I'll tell you why: it's because for centuries and across cultures, *man* has been considered a universal way to refer to humans. I mean, we do have the word *human*, but ok. Men's stories are meant to speak to all people, regardless of gender. Male pronouns are meant to be a neutral reference to a deity or to humans of all genders. Except when they refer to particular men. And when the content is clearly not intended for women's little brains, like voting, or being pastors or mechanics, or having opinions about video games and movies. That's all meant for people with penises, obviously.

If we give the men who came up with this idea the benefit of the doubt—that they really did mean all humans—even so, of course they chose *men* to be the universal term *because they were all men.* They were the ones with the power; they were the ones writing the books and making the laws. It simply never occurred to them to use something other than themselves as the model. And even though Jesus himself says we are meant to be born again (from the Spirit, from God), it would seem that the religious traditions most concerned with being born again tend also to be the ones least interested in women's leadership and divine femininity.

Does it feel like I'm being too harsh? There's a level at which I don't care—women have been told what we're allowed and not allowed to do for so damn long, a little harshness isn't so bad.

But this brings up a really important question: What is God actually like versus how we talk about God? God is like the first sunny day at the end of winter that lets us breathe deeply and realize that life is worth living. God is like the gurgling and delighted laughter of a baby. God is like a brother standing ready at our side in the face of an enemy. God is like a fierce mother storming into the principal's office to protect her daughter and all the daughters. And God is like a soothing father sitting with us in the bathroom while we're throwing up, handing over a cool cloth or gently rubbing our backs. God is so much more than any metaphor we could come up with, so much more than any word or concept could encapsulate. Our languages are so limited, there's a point we hit really quickly where we *can't* talk about God. Our words are pointlessly small, and we struggle to find just the right ones to describe what we're feeling. And so we use shorthand—God is like a father, God is like a woman searching, God is like an eagle, God is like a shirt. But God is not a father, God is not a woman searching, God is not an eagle, God is not a shirt.

This is not a new idea in the least. Throughout the big story of God and creation, God is unequivocally, unrepentantly female. And also male. (And also neither: there's a whole chapter I won't write about God as an inanimate object.) It's not that I or any other theologian is trying to make God only female, since that's patently false as well. In the same way, protesters against institutionalized racism aren't trying to make only Black lives matter. Neither is accurate or helpful. No, we are saying that God has always been spoken of in terms of all genders. It's a matter of adding rather than limiting. Black lives matter *too*; God is female *too*.

God is about desiring more—that's why she created the universe in the first place. God nursing us, teaching us, disciplining us, protecting us, snuggling us, watching us go our wayward ways, mourning when we don't listen and are hurt, rejoicing when we are found. What I'm looking for here is not an obliteration of masculine language but a raising up of feminine language—seeing *and* as a life-giving word. God is Father for those who need him to be, *and* God is also Mother for those who know they need her and for those who hadn't thought about it before. God is angry at our sin *and* made of forgiveness and forgetting. God is near *and* far, present *and* absent, massively transcendent *and* intimately immanent. Only a small god can be put in a box of one thing or another, and our God is so much bigger than that.

God contains all things. She flows like the waters of the ocean and like the sands of the desert. She is rock and tornado and soft feather bed. God is animal, mineral, and vegetable, constantly expanding and also scooting over on the couch to make room. God is black skin and white, old bones and new, female and male, simultaneously and not at all.

So I will push back hard on why it's so important that God is referred to as *he* or humans as *man* when our entire history shows us a different story, albeit a story that we have forgotten or pretend doesn't exist. How does it make us better people to think of God only in this masculine way when it is only part of who we are? Speaking of God only in masculine terms leads to *thinking* of God only in masculine terms. No amount of saying "God has a motherly side" will counteract the exclusive use of *Father* in worship.

Try this: "The Lord is my shepherd, I shall not want. She makes me lie down in green pastures and she leads me beside still waters." Or this: "Our Mother, who art in heaven, hallowed be thy name." Or this: "For God so loved the world that they gave their only Son." Does it feel a little odd in your mouth? Unpracticed? Does it feel freeing, like coming through the cut in a hill and seeing a city spread out in the valley below, all lit up in the night? It could, with practice.

God is bigger than who is in or out, beyond conservative or progressive, more spacious than Jew or Greek, slave or free, male or female. God is much more than the sum total of every human word and concept, so let's stop trying to put her in one box or the other. God is beyond binaries like the dog's trousers being worn only on the back half or the bottom half. God wears coveralls so they can get to work.

2

Sarah

Have It All, Lose It All, You Ready for More Yet?

> May the Lord judge between you and me.
> —Genesis 16:5

Long, long ago, in the faraway land of Ur, a man and a woman got married. Sarai and Abram, they were called. Mononymous before Beyoncé and Seal made it cool. We know nothing at all about their childhoods, about their courtship, even about most of their married life. The story picks up when they are old and wizened and have already lived full lives there in Ur. It was a time when the highs were high and the lows low—when all the stories told were epic, operatic, even. We do know that they were exciting and relatable (but fictional) progenitors of the Jewish people—mythic avatars, you might say.

Perhaps this is news to you that folks like Abram and Sarai, Moses and Miriam, Adam and Eve didn't exist historically. I'm sorry to be the bearer of bad news (or else I'm pleased to inform you that your suspicions were correct), but the point of so much of scripture is not that it's a historical or scientific record but that it communicates something about why God made us as we are and what God hopes for. In this case, Abraham and Sarah are flawed and fascinating character studies, heightened versions of any human ruler or parent you'd care to name. It's not an insult, and it doesn't lessen their importance when we refer to the Patriarchs and Matriarchs as metaphor or myth. Instead, it's a reminder that their stories are more than their literal meanings; they're a celebration of the depth and height of human experience. It doesn't matter that Abraham and Sarah didn't exist historically; it matters what they're telling us. And what they're telling us is that God chooses messy people to do what needs to be done; that new life constantly comes into the world, especially when it seems most full of death; and also that privilege blinds us to others' pain.

So anyway, long, long ago, in the faraway land of Ur, there were a man and a woman who got married. The woman Sarai was barren. It wasn't only on account of her being very, very old and thus well past menopause at the time of the story—it was apparently something she'd carried her whole life. Her womb was like Holly Hunter's in *Raising Arizona*, a rocky place where his seed could find no purchase. As an aside, nowhere in scripture will you find a man having "bad seed," even though every farmer would know it as a possibility. No, every time it is the woman who is broken and not able to incubate the baby the man puts in her. Sarai's barrenness, and indeed the barrenness of so many women in the Bible, is presented as fertile ground for God to do something miraculous. The women are barren *so that* God can show God's might. Never mind that infertility is a surprisingly common and emotionally devastating issue regardless of gender. If these were real people, it'd be a dick move, so I suppose this is a moment to be thankful that they're not and God's not really like this.

At their advanced ages of sixty-five and seventy-five, Sarai and her husband Abram picked up and moved because God said, in the words of my friend Alex, "I'm gonna bless you so good!" First, they moved from Ur (modern-day Iraq and Kuwait) to Haran (modern-day Turkey) and then from Haran to Canaan (the Promised Land of Exodus and modern-day Israel and Palestine).

And then, because there was a famine in Canaan (it's never really flowed with milk and honey, I'm afraid), they moved on to Egypt: on the whole, a startlingly long and intense journey for folks their age, unless those ages and others in the Torah are artificially inflated for literary purposes—which they are. There are a lot of theories from folks much more well-read than I, but they mostly mean these folks were very old and thus cosmically unlikely to have kids.

As they arrived in Egypt, and being the superstar that he was, Abram looked upon his wife and thought, *Man, look at my smokin' hot wife. The locals are totally gonna kidnap her for sexytimes and kill me in the process.* Obviously, he then told the Egyptians who met them she was his sister so that, even though Pharaoh himself did in fact kidnap her for sexytimes, Abram's life was spared, and, as we all know, that's what's really important. Perhaps it was sexytimes for Sarai, admired at her age by a powerful and exotic man, lavished with gifts and spa treatments. Perhaps it was terrifying to be used as a bargaining chip, to be powerless, to know that your partner cared so little for your well-being. Abram had no interest in her experience, no objection when Pharaoh took her away to his harem and he himself was made a wealthy man with herds of livestock in recompense. Eventually, Pharaoh and his household were stricken by plagues because of Sarai, and he said to Abram, "My dude, why did you lie about her being your sister and not your wife? Not cool. Take her and go away."

Was Sarai in on this scam? They were strangers in a strange land, refugees from famine—she may not have liked it, it might still have been traumatic, but was this plan a team effort for survival? Or was he her pimp? Nothing inappropriate happened to Sarai, right? Commenters spanning centuries have spent a lot of energy protecting her virtue. One ancient rabbi made it more palatable by saying Pharaoh only got as close as her foot and so only kept her one night. Possible, sure, but extremely unlikely. The experiences of women the world over suggest it's more likely she was a survivor of abuse and trafficking. Abram was enriched, and Sarai's body was the tool. Does this make you uncomfortable? It does me.

It is at this point—far from their original homes, far from Canaan (where they and all of scripture are aimed), and far from being the heroic, compassionate, justice-oriented people we might reasonably expect God to choose—that God made a covenant with Abram. God said, "Look up at all those stars, Abram. Can you count them? Or the grains of sand under your feet? Or the salt in the bowl on the table? That's how many kids you're gonna have." And then God told Abram to do this aesthetically gorgeous and viscerally weird ritual: Abram took a bunch of animals, cut them in half, and laid them on the ground in two rows with a path down the center—like a bloody version of the environmental artworks of Andy Goldsworthy. When he was done, Abram fell asleep. It's exhausting, butchering and making art. Also, God's works and words often come to us in dreams or even hallucinations. Abram saw God, in the form of a lit torch, moving down the path between the halved body parts. It's mystical and surreal and intense and true. You may notice that this covenant, this unbreakable vow, is with Abram only, not Sarai.

Sarai was impatient with all this promising. God said go here, they went. God said go there, they went. God said y'all are going to have a baby, but where was it? In their household was a slave named Hagar, which means "foreign thing," so it's probably not the name her parents gave her, but it tells us something about how we're supposed to read her. She is a complication in Abram and Sarai's love story with God. She brings drama and uncertainty with her from Egypt. One ancient commentary says she was Pharaoh's own daughter, given to Sarai as an apology, a reparation. Put that in your pocket for later.

Sarai took her Egyptian slave Hagar and said to Abram, "Look, I'm too old for all this shit. Take this foreign thing as a wife"—not a concubine, not a prostitute, not even a slave, but a *wife*—"and the baby y'all make will be mine." You know, like you do. Abram, bless him, didn't object to this either—sexytimes with this fetching young lady with my wife's enthusiastic consent? Where do I sign? Sarai knew God promised her husband children, but not necessarily with her. She wasn't concerned with any moral issues future readers would have with her barrenness or her decisions. She took the initiative and used what she had to hand, which happened to be another human being. I don't much care that she tried to fulfill the covenant herself—lots of folks in scripture take things into their own hands and are commended—I'm cranky about her use of Hagar's body and how she responded when it worked.

Hagar did indeed get pregnant, but the story says she looked with contempt on her sister-wife Sarai, who in turn got angry and resentful at her sister-wife Hagar. When Sarai went to Abram to complain, he again was completely uninterested in their experiences and said, "Do what you want with her." So Sarai abused Hagar. It's the same verb that Exodus uses for how the Egyptians treated Israel while they were enslaved. It's the same verb used when Shechem raped Dinah and when Amnon raped Tamar. Oppressive violence. It's not that Sarai was a little harsh; she was actively using what power she had to oppress Hagar beyond the limits of humanity. Unsurprisingly, Hagar ran away. Surprisingly, out in the wilderness, she met God face-to-face. God blessed her and called her Matriarch of her own vast family even though she was an outsider. Even more surprisingly, she returned to Sarai and Abram.

Thirteen years passed. God reiterated the covenant, this time with a fun new genital surgery for the men called circumcision! And this time, Sarai was finally included in God's favor and blessing: she and old Abe both got a name change, the addition of one of the letters in God's most sacred name Yahweh, becoming Sarah and Abraham. In this blessing, God said that their many, many, many descendants will come into being because it is Sarah, not anyone else, who will become pregnant. Who could have possibly guessed? Abraham, apparently never having considered that his wife would be the vehicle of the blessing, laughs at this: "My man, she's almost ninety. Are you serious?" I imagine Sarah listening to this and thinking, *Listen, you jerk, didn't you fear for your life because of my great beauty only a few years ago?*

Shortly afterward, they were hanging out in their tent when Abraham saw some strangers on the horizon and invited them over to have lunch. These strangers spoke in strangely certain and otherworldly voices, and they, too, pronounced that Sarah would have a baby. And then it was Sarah's turn to laugh. I mean, she may have been a hot old lady, and her husband a little on the clueless side, but honestly, it's a natural reaction for both of them. She said to herself, maybe with disbelief, maybe with wonder, "I am so old. Will I have pleasure again?" I am delighted to tell you that in Hebrew, it says, "I am old and dried up, will there still be for me wetness?" I love this so very much: it's a metaphor for life in the desert and for the feeling of being old and done. It's a metaphor for the delight of having children, but it's also a metaphor for a woman's arousal. Women's pleasure and wetness are not spoken of much in scripture—I can think of one other place, in the Song of Songs, when the woman speaks of masturbating and going to answer the door while her hands are still wet. And we certainly don't talk about that kind of thing in church, yet here it is, not only in the Bible but as a part of one of our major origin stories. We remember that Sarah laughed, but do we remember it's because she might have been thinking about orgasm?

The strangers said, "Why did you laugh?" She said, "I didn't." They said, "Oh, yes, you did," and I wonder what the tone of voice was meant to be. Was it kind of a shaming "you should know God can do impossible things" kind of moment? Many male commenters have taken this tack: "Sarah, sweetheart, is anything too difficult or too wonderful for God? Get ahold of yourself." They didn't say the same things of Abraham laughing only a chapter before. Or was it a kind tone, delight for her delight? Like Dora the Explorer and Boots the monkey dancing and shouting, "A baby, a baby, a baby!"

In what seems like a poor editorial decision, we then get another version of the "you're so hot, pretend to be my sister so they don't kill me when they kidnap you for sexytimes" story. (For those counting at home, this is the second of three iterations of this story. The last one is perpetrated by Isaac on Rebekah later on.) This time, it's King Abimelech who is the dupe and within the text itself is the protection for Sarah's virtue, as Abimelech had some sort of vague disease that prevented him from touching her. Hooray, it could have been worse. Then Abimelech, an outsider to this chosen family who will become the Israelite nation, within the sacred text of that fledgling nation, told Abraham he's done wrong. Abraham was the sinner here. Abraham offered a bunch of excuses including the revelation that in fact he wasn't truly lying, since she was *literally his half sister* and God made him wander and it's so hard so you, Abimelech, should be nice to me. Here I imagine Abimelech rolling his eyes and shoving a bunch of livestock and money at him and saying, "My dude, not cool. Please just go." Interestingly, this particular version of the story ends with Abraham actually being the blessing God has blessed him to be and praying for the healing of Abimelech and his household. It works, though they were only cursed with this vague disease because Abraham let them take his wife. Sister. Whatever.

Which brings me to Sarah and Abraham's shared father Terah. Scholars differ wildly on whether this kind of incestuous marriage would have been accepted or taboo. Ancient myths the world over include close family sexual relationships because, honestly, there weren't enough people yet to have other options. Genesis 4 tells us Cain was exiled to the area east of Eden and married there—where did his wife come from if there had only been four humans until then? Noah's nuclear family were the only people spared in the flood, and they apparently repopulated the earth. These stories sound ridiculous when read from a literal angle because that's not how we're supposed to read them. I don't want to downplay real-life incest, but these ancestral stories are told from a place of why, not how. They're about God's care for our people, whoever "our people" might be. Should we feel icky about their familial relationships now? I can't answer for you, but probably not.

When Isaac was finally born, Sarah and Abraham were filled with genuine joy. I think they named him Isaac, famously meaning "laughter," both as a sly reference to their disbelief that this thing could happen and also after their sheer rapture. Can you imagine at ninety and one hundred (or whatever advanced ages they actually were) holding their widdle baby Isaac with his widdle baby toes and his widdle baby ears and not laughing? He was a miracle in every sense of the word. Though, to be clear, they did go about making and having him in the usual way. God made it happen, but, you know, so did they. You might say it was a group project.

And following directly on the heels of this great rapture was great cruelty. Sarah saw the foreign thing Hagar's boy Ishmael playing with little Isaac in the yard, and she couldn't stand it. Calling her a slave rather than a wife, she threw Hagar and her son out of the camp into the wilderness. Many people have remarked on the similarity between Sarah and white slaveholding women in the United States, between Hagar and the women used by their mistresses' husbands. Maybe now is a good time to mention that God works not with perfect people but through the people who are around. As Arthur Ashe said, "Start where you are, use what you have, do what you can." Sarah and Abraham were far from perfect, but they were there.

There follows one of the most horrible and most told stories in scripture, Abraham's almost-sacrifice of Isaac. You can read volumes about that elsewhere, but let me just say this about that: there are many scholars across the generations who believe that Abraham made a mistake here and that the story isn't about Abraham's great faithfulness but about God's provision. I love this reading. Rather than assuming that Abraham then and we now are meant to blindly follow whatever commands we hear as divine, no matter how hurtful they might be, God steps in to turn us in a different direction. Notice, it's not that God fixes everything like a divine mechanic—Abraham still killed the ram to gain God's favor, which he presumably already had—but God kind of shifts our focus like a new pair of glasses so we can see some of the bigger picture.

What's even more interesting to me is how this story butts up immediately against the next one: Sarah's death. The story goes that after Sarah died, Abraham mourned and wept and negotiated his first official purchase of land in Canaan for her grave. Why put them right next to each other? Why edit it in this particular way? Sarah is not present in the story of almost-sacrifice at all—did Abe think, *My wife will be so mad if she knows what I'm about to do*, and just didn't tell her until after it all turned out fine? The one following the other suggests she died of grief and shock, as any good heroine might before 1900. Maybe her death right after the almost-sacrifice suggests Abraham should have thought through his actions—all of them—a little more. Maybe her death mythically represents the death of the relationship between her husband and son—Isaac was spared, but there was a cost; there's always a cost. Or maybe Sarah's death invites us to look back at her son's life, given to her as a surprising gift and a reprieve for her emptiness and later given back to him as a gift and a delight and a consolation. New life continuing in the midst of mourning.

Sarah is not an easy person to summarize. Her life doesn't wrap up with a neat little bow. She's lighthearted and faithful, mythic and relatable, victim and oppressor, all at the same time. What's the word for having privilege in one space but not in another, for being both an insider and an outsider simultaneously, for the cruelty we absorb from those with power over us and then unleash on others more helpless than we are? What's the word for when you have it all and lose it all simultaneously? This is Sarah. Consider a highly respected Black church matron who is in charge of every committee—even the pastor quakes a little when she sails into his office in her Sunday best. Consider the deference from younger people in the church, from people in the neighborhood. And consider her begging a white judge for lenience for her son who'd been arrested. Imagine the weight and the pull and the powerlessness of that inside her. Sarah is respected, the oldest and greatest of the Matriarchs, clearly a woman to be reckoned with. And she was the victim of her husband and Pharaoh and the male-centric society in which she lived. And she used the weapons of her own oppressors against Hagar, who had even less standing than she. Why didn't Sarah recognize the similarity of their situations? Why didn't she choose solidarity and sisterhood instead of rejection? Because even she, Matriarch Sarai, was afraid of losing everything she had.

Aren't we all? These particular people didn't exist, but they feel so much like us. They reflect back to us our own fear of losing what we have, our own pleasure when new possibilities come into being, our own taking advantage of others. We're just as messy as Sarah was, just as oblivious as Abraham was. The point of these stories, it seems to me, is God's presence with them along their entire journey. Whatever choices they made, God walked alongside them. To paraphrase Thich Nhat Hanh, when they walked, they arrived in God's presence with every step. God was never not there, nudging, hoping, sometimes demanding. That doesn't mean God approved of the manner of their walking, that God was pleased with every decision they made. It means that they and we are never alone. It means that every single step we take has the possibility of new life, even when it feels most full of death. It doesn't matter that they didn't exist historically; what they mean is much more important. God chooses messy people, people who hurt and disappoint, not perfect people, because we're the only kinds of people there are.

3

Rachel and Leah (and Bilhah and Zilpah)

> When Rachel saw that she bore Jacob no children, she envied her sister; and she said to Jacob, "Give me children, or I shall die!"
>
> —GENESIS 30:1

There's a prayer we use in the Episcopal Church when we bless the bread and wine that talks about "the vast expanse of interstellar space, galaxies, suns, the planets in their courses, and this fragile earth, our island home." It's officially named Prayer C, but we lovingly call it the Star Wars Prayer. It's beautiful and soul lifting and I love it very much. Anyway, whenever I am presiding at Eucharist and we use that prayer, I get a little irritated with the writers because, near the end, there's a bit describing God with an ancient but incomplete formulation: "Lord God of our Fathers: God of Abraham, Isaac, and Jacob." Jews and Christians have been using this name for God for millennia, but it's missing something, missing *someone*: the Mothers Sarah, Rebekah, Leah, and Rachel. And Bilhah and Zilpah, now we come to it. I insert all their names every time with their appropriate spouses, and it feels like I'm winning something. Yeah, I remembered all their names without writing it down; yeah, I said them out loud. It's a little clunky but satisfying—these women are just as important to the story as their husbands.

There was a woman named Rachel who was very beautiful. Not as beautiful as Queen Esther or the widow Judith, but still a fine figure of a woman. Her older sister Leah was also lovely. Or possibly unsightly. The Hebrew word is enigmatic, literally "tender eyed," and is translated variously as dull, weak, peculiar, and lovely. Come on, Bible, get your shit together. Scholar Wilda Gafney wonders if the word isn't about how she looked but about how she *saw*. Either way, the two of them were rivals, according to the story, competing for the love of Jacob, son of Isaac, son of Abraham. Their three-point relationship was as uncertain as Leah's eyes.

Rachel met Jacob first. He had come to her town from far away because his mother Rebekah wanted him to find a wife from their extended family. He seems to have taken her literally because when he stopped at the well near Rachel's house, she was the first woman he saw, and he literally fell down weeping at her feet and kissed her cheeks. Just a little dramatic, that one. She was all sweaty, grass in her hair and smelling of sheep because she was a shepherd, the only shepherd in scripture identified as female. What if it had been Leah there at the well instead, twisting together cords for rope or bringing stew and news to the shepherds? Would her eyes and her whole being have had a less enigmatic meaning? Would she have been the one Jacob kissed through tears?

When Rachel and Jacob returned to her house, her father Laban also kissed Jacob, saying, "Brother, we are kinfolk. Take your coat off and stay a while," and so Jacob stayed for twenty years. It started off as a month of hospitality and conversation, maybe some casual flirting with Rachel and/or Leah. Eventually, Jacob got around to his reason for being there: "Laban, my friend, I am meant to take a wife, and I would very much like that wife to be your Rachel." Laban returned, "Certainly, Jacob, my friend, I need help around the farm, and I would very much like you to do it for the next seven years." And so the two men struck a bargain—Jacob's labor for Rachel's hand, Rachel's opinion not being solicited or recorded.

"That's not entirely fair," you might be saying. "The story skims over a lot of things, and you're assuming they didn't talk to her—what if she was madly in love with Jacob and asking her dad every evening when he would offer her to him?" It's entirely possible, but historically, her opinion was immaterial. Women, and specifically women's bodies, have long been bargaining chips and links among male-led families, whether or not they were interested. There are countless examples of royals marrying off their children to cement political alliances and of poor families, too, handing over their daughters, often simply to lessen the number of mouths to feed. I'm reminded of a fan fiction story where Harry Potter and Draco Malfoy (yes, that Harry and Draco) were ambassadors to the fairies, but it went wrong, and only marrying off Draco to a fairy prince would unruffle feathers, even though he was clearly in love with Harry. I know, fiction not history, but reflective that consent, enthusiastic or not, has nothing to do with it.

So Jacob worked for Laban for seven years, mucking out stables, helping the sheep and goats give birth, planting and harvesting, all with his eyes on Rachel and Leah's eyes on him.

When the time came for them to be married, Jacob went into the wedding tent thinking of his love Rachel, thinking of making good on the promises of their flirting. Under cover of darkness, it was Leah who lay there, nervous that he would see her, longing for him to. He made sweet, sweet love to his wife, and it was everything he had dreamed of. In the light of morning, he rolled over to gaze at Rachel's face and saw that it was Leah looking back, pleasure and fear both in her eyes. Of course, Jacob stormed off to yell at Laban—why the deception? Hadn't he just worked seven years for Rachel? Was he even married to Leah? Their argument could be heard all over town, people clucking their tongues, saying, "Laban's at it again." Some say Laban was greedy and wanted more work out of Jacob, others that he was a zealot for marrying off the eldest first, a tradition that hadn't been mentioned until just this moment. Or maybe Rachel had something to do with the switch.

She was just as tricksy as Laban and Jacob—it could be she wasn't interested and she and Leah made a pact, conflict put aside for the moment. Surely the two of them were at least aware of the plan somewhere along the way. The narrator doesn't much care about anyone's feelings on the matter other than Jacob wanting Rachel. It's another of scripture's frustratingly ambiguous moments.

Laban said, "Let's call it an even fourteen years between friends and you can have them both." ("Oh, and these two other servants, Zilpah and Bilhah—the girls can have them too. I'm done with them.") So Jacob worked another seven years, weeding and digging and shearing and milking, all with his eyes on Rachel and his wife Leah's eyes on him.

Leah, the story says, was hated. That is, she was unloved, passed over, unseen. *Hated* seems like a strong word—maybe Jacob and Rachel did hate her, maybe she experienced his lack of interest as hatred. But the story says because she felt hated, God saw her and made her fruitful—she had four sons in quick and heartbreaking succession. Leah, bless her, became increasingly desperate for Jacob's love even as she seemed to have him regularly in her bed. She named her sons Reuben (meaning "Look! A son! Do you love me, husband?"), Simeon (meaning "God hears me because I am hated,"), Levi (meaning "Surely he'll stay with me this time"), and Judah (meaning "This time I'll praise God because no one else is paying attention").

In the meantime, Rachel was having her own desperate crisis—she was younger than Leah, and she and Jacob were making so much sweet love, but nothing was happening. She was barren. (Again with scripture blaming the woman for infertility, I swear.) Like so many women before her, she hoped a baby would change things. Rachel was just as dramatic as Jacob and said to him, "If you don't give me a damn baby, I'll die!" He yelled back that it wasn't his fault God hadn't given her a baby yet. Neither of them, you might notice, bothered to consult God's opinion on the matter. Rachel, mimicking her grandmother Sarah, handed Jacob her maid Bilhah and said, "Take her as your wife, then. Go make your sweet love to her and I'll have her babies as my own." And Jacob said, "Fine!" And Rachel said, "Fine!" And no one asked Bilhah what she thought because she was just the maid. Rachel held Bilhah's first in triumph and named him Dan (meaning "God judged me righteous") and again her second son and named him Naphtali (meaning "I wrestled with my sister for years and now I've won!").

Then it ceased to be with Leah in the way of women (she hit menopause), so in order to still be competitive with Rachel, she handed Jacob *her* maid Zilpah and said, "You know what to do." Jacob said nothing at all, really, because he seemed to just be a walking baby maker at this point in the story. Zilpah bore two sons whom Leah named Gad (meaning "Heck yeah, what great fortune!") and Asher (meaning "I'm so happy. Don't I look happy to you?"). Look, I'm sure she was happy in some ways—she was fulfilling her cultural purpose, she had many strapping boys to take care of her in her old age, she was well ahead of Rachel in the point totals, and she even loved her little boys—but these names feel a bit strained, like she was trying to convince herself or lean into the children rather than Jacob.

When her eldest Reuben ("Look! A son!") found mandrake out in the fields, a plant that was supposed to magically increase fertility and arousal, Rachel traded Jacob himself away for the night to get some of it to make her body make a baby. Leah met Jacob that night, saying, "I've bought and paid for you. You're coming with me"—it literally says that—to which Jacob again replied with nothing. And Leah miraculously bore two more sons, Issachar (meaning "I paid for this one") and Zebulun (meaning "Jacob will honor me because of all the sons I've given him" or possibly "cohabitation") as a result, and as an afterthought, a daughter Dinah, whose name is not given a meaning in the text but which means "judged" or "vindicated." You can read *The Red Tent* to find out why.

At long last, Rachel got pregnant, perhaps as a result of the mandrake's magic, and named her son Joseph, meaning "Ach, finally, and how about another?" While we're discussing names, you might be interested to hear that Rachel's name means "ewe" and Leah's means "cow." Lovely.

Who's winning at this point? It's hard to say—Rachel was still the preferred wife, but Leah had more children. Bilhah and Zilpah, though they're both called *isshah*, meaning "actual wife," not "concubine" or "maid," have definitely never caught up. They all reached a détente for a time because the family was leaving Laban's house: Jacob, a trickster himself, was disgusted with Laban's dirty tricks over the last fourteen years and ready to go home; Leah and Rachel were disgusted with their dad's having sold them like livestock and wasted whatever wealth they might have inherited. No one asked Bilhah and Zilpah what they thought. Perhaps they were disgusted too.

So Jacob did a little sheep magic: having made yet another bargain with Laban that Jacob would only take the mottled sheep and goats from the flock, not the pure-colored ones, and Laban cheating yet again by taking all the mottled sheep far away from the camp, Jacob whittled some branches so they looked spotted, then made sure the sheep and goats could see them when they went to make their sweet, sheepy love—and presto, lots of mottled sheep and goat babies. It's just science, folks.

This operation took a few years, as gestation is not a quick process, and you would think Laban would catch on to the sheep-magic cheating going on, but once Jacob had just a shit ton of mottled ungulates (meaning "hooved animals," and I am charmed to learn it's a category that also includes hippos and dolphins), they left Laban's quickly. In the scramble to leave, Rachel snuck into her father's house and stole his household gods—not just a personal affront but a taking of power. Rachel had always been something of a main character, not a secondhand, unseen woman, and in taking these gods, she was claiming leadership and power for herself. Laban came after them, ostensibly to say goodbye to his loving daughters but clearly to recover the totems of his power and stability and to show his strength. He and Jacob circled each other like predators, like Leah and Rachel used to do. Hilariously,

Rachel hid the household gods in her camel's saddle and then sat on it, claiming with a wink and a nudge that the way of women was upon her. I love the glee with which Rachel must have articulated her menstruation to her clueless and dismayed father. What a simple thing to repel a man by discussing natural processes.

The two men ended up making certain guarantees that they would stay away from each other and that Jacob would neither abuse Laban's daughters nor marry even more wives. Perhaps this is the only time Laban truly saw Leah and Rachel as something other than commodities. Even so, their covenant was not as sentimental as the famous line, "May God watch between you and me when we are absent from one another," might suggest. God's watching between them is a threat.

There follows the famous scene of Jacob wrestling with an angel-who-is-also-somehow-God and walking away wounded and blessed. Even with God's blessing on him, Jacob then panicked that his brother Esau was on the way to destroy him and all he had, so he put his wives and children at the farthest point of their caravan to protect them, with Rachel and Joseph the farthest away and thus most protected—another point for Rachel.

After all of this—after all the fighting, all the childbearing, all the trickery, all the years living in and out of each other's pockets—Rachel died on the road. She was pregnant with her second child, "great with child" they used to say, and she went into labor during the journey. As she pushed and panted, crouching on the bricks, clinging to Bilhah and Leah and Zilpah, she wept, feeling her own end coming even as she created a beginning. Through her tears, she named her son Benjamin, "son of my sorrow." I can't bear to make a comical version of this name, this cry of grief in the space between one life and another. In the end, Rachel was buried by herself in the wilderness, and Leah was buried with Jacob. In the end, Leah won.

Oh, and parenthetically, there's the sad tale, more of a mention, really, of Leah's eldest Reuben raping his stepmother Bilhah. Some say it wasn't actually sex, that Jacob began preferring Bilhah after

Rachel's death, and Reuben was only sticking up for his mom by moving Bilhah's bed out of Jacob's tent. Some say Bilhah was "embroiled" with Reuben, encouraging his advances or at least mutually desirous. Who could blame her? A young, vigorous man set to inherit wealth and power, and she, still in her own youth or perhaps older and flattered by his attention, never having gotten to choose her own lover. Little is said about it and little comes of it. All that it might have meant to her is contained within the parentheses.

So much of these women's stories is parenthetical—their feelings and desires unimportant, their lives outside of childbearing unseen, not necessary to the bigger story being told. As much as Leah and Rachel's story is about competition, I think it's about something deeper, something more essential to their beings and ours. These women, all four of them, longed to be seen. They longed for Jacob's attention, certainly, but their anger with their father might suggest they longed for his as well. Like children on the playground saying, "Look at me, Dad!" they say, "See the thing I made; see what I'm excited about. Don't waste your time and money on others. Look at me!" They didn't even receive divine name changes when Jacob did, like their grandmother Sarah did. Bilhah and Zilpah were handed over to new mistresses as afterthoughts to the main plotline. They had no voice, no say in what happened to them. Perhaps they found Jacob's household and bed preferable to Laban's, perhaps not. They were not considered Matriarchs like their sister-wives, even though the text says they are on the same level. They were, as I referred to myself when pregnant, factories to build babies.

And yet the women in this story are incredibly visible, vocal, and necessary to the continuation of the Israelite people. Jacob's father Isaac had to be born from Sarah for the story and the promise to work, Jacob himself was his mother Rebekah's favorite, Bilhah and Zilpah were servants with no stories of their own but are listed a generation later alongside Leah and Rachel as progenitors of Israel, Matriarchs in deed if not word. The twelve tribes of Israel were first the longed-for babies of Jacob's four wives, their great-ness and their destiny to number as the stars came from these women's wombs. They wrestled with the men around them for every scrap of visibility and power.

The power dynamics Black people experience and shape in the United States pivot around the same need to be seen. Their humanity, their inner lives, their plans and hopes have been ignored ever since white folks decided they needed free labor and called them slaves. Who they actually were was rendered invisible to render tangible their labor and their fearsomeness. False nar-ratives claiming their insensitivity to pain, their innate violence, their love of being ordered around were created to justify greed and cruelty. But it is they who have urged our country forward, who have created, almost ex nihilo, the freedom we actually enjoy. Nikole Hannah-Jones wrote in her famous essay "The 1619 Proj-ect," "Our democracy's founding ideals were false when they were written. Black Americans have fought to make them true." We didn't truly see founding ideals for generations, but like Leah and Rachel, they have made us see them.

Leah and Rachel and Bilhah and Zilpah make visible women's lives, women's desires to be loved and recognized and fulfilled. They make visible the cost women pay and the work women do and the lengths women go for the larger story to exist. The show must go on, and even if the eyes of the public are on the male stars, their work is meaningless without the women on stage with them, behind the scenes, selling tickets, and sweeping up after. Just to be abundantly clear, it's not that women are only, must only be, in supportive roles—that's a bald-faced lie made up to keep power where it is. No, it's that we have a film over our own eyes and couldn't see them right in front of us, like the special-effects crew painted them out. They've been there all along, though, taking up space, soliloquizing, causing chaos, and walking with God right alongside the men. And so are we.

When I read this story, I think of the movie *The Favourite*, the one with Olivia Colman, Emma Stone, and Rachel Weisz.

Gosh, they're all so good. It's about these two noblewomen feuding over their lover, the queen, with glances and suggestions and outright trickery. One of them eventually triumphs over the other, but it's no victory. The last shot is her dreadful realization of what she has actually won. What they wanted was power in a world of chaos, being seen by the woman instigating chaos. What Leah and Rachel and Bilhah and Zilpah wanted wasn't so much the power as the power of being seen, of knowing that their desires and needs were allowed, were welcomed. What we want now is the same: the power to change the chaos around us, our desires and needs being validated, to be recognized, to be understood, not to be invisible.

I look at the cool people around me, the people who have their shit together, the people who are doing talented and transformative things, and I feel like Leah, longing for them to look at me with love, longing to be enough. I look at other campus ministries or other entire denominations in the church, and I feel like Rachel, envious of their success, their numbers, their seeming ease. I find myself competing for competency and for the spotlight while simultaneously simply wanting to be known. I can't win campus ministry, I can't win the feeling of ease, and I can't force people to know me or see me. But I can learn to see myself with Leah's tender eyes; I can learn to work within the constraints around me like Rachel, to be a bit tricksy in the process.

In Jewish mysticism, these four women are collectively referred to as *barzel*, meaning "iron." Their initials make up the letters of the word, and their souls form a strong framework for our lives. They are representatives of God's presence in conflict—not waiting until it is resolved and not even resolving it—simply being their whole selves, going after what they want, mourning their losses, adjusting to new situations, trying to function and do better each day than the day before. These iron women are a community of faith in the shape of a family, venerable and awkward and blessed, saying to us across the generations as we grieve and create and wonder, "Look, a son! Look, a daughter!"

4

Miriam

To the World We Dream about and the One We Live in Now

But you blew with your breath,
and the sea covered them.
They sank like lead
in the mighty waters.

—Exodus 15:10 (NIV)

It was a long time ago and the people still worshipped many gods: Asherah and Baal, definitely El, probably the brand-new one Yahweh, though maybe that one was older than the rest? And some people called God Adonai. Anyway, it was a long time ago and the people who'd come from the family of Jacob were far, far from their homeland. It had started by necessity. There was a famine, and their youngest son had somehow become the fancy manager of all of Egypt, so they went there to survive. And then it just got comfortable, like things do, and it was home. But there was a new king, a new pharaoh there in Egypt who had forgotten Joseph and Jacob and only saw them as filthy foreigners or hadn't known or cared to begin with. And so they were slaves, in exile from even the idea of home.

It was a dark time. To be fair, it was also a bright, sunny, warm time as well, what with Egypt's climate. Disgustingly beautiful, actually, considering their state of slavery. Like visiting the site of a concentration camp, the walls and the ground saturated with misery, the air stinking of pain and shit, but the sky cloudless and blue and a light breeze blowing the sound of birdsong into your open ears. It was like that.

The people needed a change. They were bitter and anxious and beaten down. They needed salvation, a hero, a hope. And so a woman named Jochebed had a baby boy. This is not his story, not really. The story begins with his birth, so you're forgiven for thinking it's about him. His is the story we know, whose tagline "Let my people go" was said with a stammer and a glinting-toothed smile. He seems to be at the center of this hope for change, and he is the one who gets all the credit. And, like many a billionaire or war hero or beloved pop-culture icon, he did not do it all by himself, possibly not much of it at all. The story we know is about Moses. The story I'm going to tell you is about Miriam, his sister.

Miriam was the firstborn, not that it got her anything, since only boys mattered. She was well aware of this, and she'd made a little peace with it. After all, boys were fun even if she couldn't imagine why her little brother Aaron got all the best meat and didn't have to do the mending. But at ten years old, Miriam didn't take it lying down either. Her family and her friends, everyone she knew as a young girl, were tired. They worked long hours in the hot sun making bricks for King Pharaoh, whoever he was, to build big, fancy buildings in his own honor. Once from a distance she caught a glimpse of him on his chariot—that's what someone told her it was called—his big, fancy, gold cart thing. He looked rich and angry and not hungry. She thought he looked like he was trying too hard. Everyone she knew said they had to do what King Pharaoh said or else they would die. Miriam remembered the story about how God told the first people they had to not eat from one tree or else they would die. But they didn't then, did they? Maybe they wouldn't now. Miriam, she was full of questions.

When her mom got pregnant, everyone was scared. Miriam knew why. She knew King Pharaoh said all the baby boys were supposed to be killed. But she didn't know why King Pharaoh was so afraid of babies. She'd heard that the midwives were supposed to kill the boy babies, but they'd lied to King Pharaoh and kept them hidden away—she didn't know if it was true, but those midwives were heroes in her eyes. *Good for them*, she thought. What was wrong with him that a bunch of fat little poop machines frightened him? But it didn't matter in the end because she saw, peeking around windows and hiding under furniture, the soldiers come. She saw them rip her neighbors' sons from their arms and run them through with swords. She smelled the blood and heard the screams and, worse, later, the whimpers that filled the night of parents with empty arms. When she went down to the river to collect water, she hadn't thought about what she would find until she saw the small bodies floating past like toy boats. She sat down, hugged her knees, and stared, her sadness and anger so hot that her tears dried up. Who did King Pharaoh think he was? Why was he allowed to do this? Adonai, how could you allow something like this?

Jochebed's pregnancy wasn't intentional, but these things happen even in the worst of times. And it's unclear if this baby was Miriam's half brother or brother—the writers and editors of scripture didn't care much, or they erased the bits that explained it. She felt protective of this new brother, and mother and daughter hatched a plan. Jochebed had the baby in the usual way, crouched on the bricks, one of the midwives holding her shoulders and encouraging her. And they washed him down and stuck a breast in his mouth just as he began to cry. Jochebed looked at his scrunched-up, red face and cried for the world they found themselves in, the world that wasn't good enough for her children. And then she swaddled him up tight as he drifted off into milk-sleep and put him in a basket she'd woven for him to sleep in. She and Miriam snuck down to the river and settled the basket along the side among the rushes. They stared at him for a few moments, lost in thought. Maybe they thought of all the other babies they'd seen floating in the river. Maybe they prayed to Adonai for protection. And then they turned and left him.

What was the plan, though? Did they know King Pharaoh's daughter would be hanging out at that particular part of the river? Were they hoping to pop down there several times a day to change his nappies and feed him? Or did they think it might be a better death than a sword to be surrounded by green rushes and blue sky? I don't know and the writers don't enlighten us. But the princess showed up and cooed over him and decided to adopt this cute foreign baby—perhaps she thought to rescue him from savagery as so many powerful women have, or perhaps she'd seen her father's violent narcissism and wanted nothing to do with it. Miriam had been watching, and she was a sharp cookie—she ran up to the princess and asked, all innocent, "Do you need someone to nurse that baby?" When the princess said yes, Miriam brought back her mom, the baby's mom, to be the wet nurse. Some folks say the princess was so grateful for all of this, she later named a daughter Miriam. A bizarre turn of events, but there you have it. The princess named the baby Moses, and off we go.

Or, rather, off Moses goes. We hear nothing about his sister until after Moses murdered someone, after he heard voices from a brush fire, after he stammered his way through ten horrifying and truly over-the-top plagues, and after his staff split the Reed Sea and the Israelites walked through on dry ground. (If you're confused, we call it the Red Sea, but that's a misreading or mishearing of its real name.) Miriam was around, she was doing stuff—Exodus suggests she was close to ninety years old when they crossed the Reed Sea, a venerable and authoritative matron, or a spring chicken, if the stories about Sarah's beauty at that age are to be believed—we just don't know about it. But once they crossed the sea, once the Egyptian slave masters were destroyed by walls of water, then Miriam stood on the shore, staring at the bodies of men and horses floating by, and remembered another time and place. Her sadness and anger were so hot that her tears dried up. But instead of hugging her knees, she lifted her tambourine and she sang. Miriam sang about death and destruction; she sang a song of delight and ferocious triumph that her family, her people, had survived and their oppressors had died, every last one, crushed by the sea. She and all the women sang and danced, lifting their voices, writing new and more violent verses, more thankful and passionate verses, to their freedom song. The men joined in, all the people singing Miriam's song. Miriam sang, and she was called a prophet. And later, when they wrote it down, her words were given to Moses. She kept only a couple of lines, after the fact, as though her pain and triumph were nothing. Deborah got to keep her violent, triumphant song later—why didn't Miriam?

Miriam was the first person to be named a prophet in the Hebrew scriptures, rather like Mary Magdalene was the first to tell the good news of Jesus' resurrection. Was her prophecy her truth-telling and celebration? Was it the work she did among the people, leading them and teaching them while Moses was off finding himself? Did she have a direct experience of God calling like her brother and the prophets after her? What I wouldn't give to read an account of that conversation. Maybe one day long ago, she sat by the river near her house, hugging her knees and staring at the water, remembering. And a Person sat next to her for a time, not speaking, sharing her grief. Maybe the Person said quietly but with lightning in their voice, "Miriam, you will lead these people; you will tell them of God and of the hope they have." Maybe Miriam turned to look at the Person who was maybe also God and, with a contemplative head-tilt, said, "Oh, yeah? Why?" Maybe they talked for a while on the bank of that river until the sky was streaked with red and orange and clouds like paste and then Miriam said, "Let it be with me as you say." Maybe.

It's a heavy title, "prophet." From what we know, the prophets were people of authority but also not people who most folks wanted to be around all the time. Prophets were truth tellers, not soothsayers, though in English, those words are a hair's breadth apart. They told truths that many would rather have kept quiet. Prophets saw the world for what it was, not with a Pollyanna-ish charm and not with a Nostradamus-like prediction but clearly and now, with all its faults and beauty alike. They weren't married, mostly (Huldah was, Ezekiel was a widower, and Hosea might have been), and the mantle of prophet was something not many women wore. It was hard for (typically male) religious leaders for centuries afterward to wrap their minds around Miriam being a prophet. They seem vexed by her lack of spouse and kids, so they try to marry her off to various men including Caleb, a helpful bit of fix-it fan fiction that ties her to David. They say she convinced her parents to stay together and have a baby despite King Pharaoh because she foresaw the coming of Moses. And she is named in more biblical books than any other woman: all the Marys in the Christian Testament are named after her, and there are so, so many Miriams in midrash and the Talmud.

But she disappears from the story again, just when we could really use her presence. The people wandered in the desert, complaining, frustrated with this new normal. They were thirsty, but the water was brackish, so Moses talked to God and sweetened it. They were hungry, so Moses talked to God and got them quails and manna (which is my most favorite word in scripture. It literally means "What is it?" The Israelites were told to go out and gather this papery grain thing that appeared on the ground like dew, and their first thought was, *What is it?* I so identify with them.) They got thirsty again, so Moses talked to God and made water from a rock. Miriam was there with them, but she's absent from the text. Where was Miriam?

This dude Amalek picked a fight with them out there in the wilderness—not as empty a place as you might think—and there was a great battle. Moses promised that as long as his staff was held up in the air, the Israelites would win—that's a science fact, my friends. So two of his most trusted leaders stood nearby and held his arms up for the entire battle: one, his dear brother, who had been with him through thick and thin, and the other, some guy named Hur. They said, centuries later, that Hur was Miriam's son with Caleb. Where was Miriam?

Finally, they arrived at Mount Sinai and God appeared to them, as was fashionable at the time, as a terrifying lightning storm on top of the mountain. Moses hiked up into the cloud and received the Ten Commandments as well as a bunch of other commandments and an incredibly specific and fabulous interior design scheme for the tabernacle, a moveable, tent-based house for God. He was up there for forty days and forty nights, and Aaron and that guy Hur were with the people, guiding them. Where was Miriam?

And while Moses was up there communing with God, what were the people up to? They got bored and they turned to Aaron—trusted, righteous, helpful Aaron—and they said, "You know what would be neat? Make us a cow out of gold, and we'll worship that!" And he did. No objections, no pause. Aaron immediately took all their jewelry, melted it down, and made a statue of a calf for them to dance around. I mean, I get the boredom particularly here in 2020, but also, God was literally at the top of the mountain in the form of a scary lightning storm: actual God was *right there*. Where, I ask you, was Miriam?

After Moses came down from his mountaintop retreat, after he threw down and broke the lovely, carved stone tablets with the commandments and the other commandments and the interior designs, after he had Aaron and all of his family murder three thousand of their already precariously small group because of the calf, he went back up and did it all again, minus the calf and murder. This time, they spend several chapters actually making the fabulous tabernacle. And this time, Moses' face shone like a lightbulb because he'd been speaking with God. Was Miriam surprised by all this? Wasn't he just her annoying little brother? Where was Miriam?

We don't see her again until partway through Numbers, when she and Aaron were annoyed by Moses having married outside the family. Exciting stuff, that. To be fair, if we're to believe the genealogy, Moses and maybe Aaron and Miriam are all the children of incest because their dad Amram married his Auntie Jochebed.

Much of the Hebrew scripture is concerned with marrying within the tribe, within their own people (though not this closely), which makes sense when you're a smallish group and it's pivotal that you keep your customs and your possessions: they're your very identity. Endogamy, they call it, and Miriam and Aaron were fans. But Moses had gone off and married Zipporah of Midian, an outsider. Maybe their distaste came from her being an outsider to the life and culture they knew. Maybe it had to do with the baffling incident years earlier when Moses was bringing her and their son back to the wandering group and God tried to kill him while they were stopped overnight at a motel, so Zipporah circumcised their son and then waved the foreskin at Moses' own penis and, magically, God backed off. I'm not kidding, both about that story being in the Bible and about centuries of scholars being baffled about it. It's baffling.

Whatever the case, they all went to the tent of meeting to bring it up with God. Aaron and Miriam both asked, "Is Moses the only one God has given authority to? No, of course not. You know it; we know it." And God—hearing Aaron and Miriam's concern and being aware, as the text says, that Moses was the most humble person on the face of the earth—appeared to them as the pillar of cloud and said, "Listen, you're great and all, but you can't question what my boy Moses says or does. Period." A bit dangerous, the idea that any one person in authority can't ever be questioned, but then the cloud dissipated, and Miriam was covered all over with a gross skin disease that turned her white and crusty. Notice: *Miriam*, not *Aaron and Miriam*, though they both spoke up. Some interpreters say that originally, it was only Miriam who questioned Moses, so she was justly punished for her sass, but if you read the story, Aaron is embedded in it—it's clearly not just her. She got to be healed—hooray—but not until she was shut out of the camp for seven days to be purified, physically and ritually.

Eventually, we come across the last part of Miriam's story, her death. It is reported in the text with no fanfare. But what's fascinating is what comes directly after: "Now there was no water for the congregation." Immediately after she died, there was no water. They've somehow had water since that time way back when Moses got water from the rock, and now they don't. The water was bitter and then it was sweet. They were thirsty and then they had plenty to drink. There's a story, another bit of fan fiction, that gets told about this, that it wasn't Moses who brought water from the rock; it was Miriam. And somehow, that rock—as a giant boulder, as a fountain, as a sieve—followed the people for their years of wandering in the wilderness. Miriam's Well, it's called in rabbinic literature. First, the water was bitter, *marah* in Hebrew and also the root word of Miriam's name. "Bitter water woman," she's sometimes called, but also "beloved" in Egyptian. Even her name is a question. And when she died, the water dried up. Her presence, her energy, her authority kept them alive for years.

Miriam was there in a bunch of the big moments like Mary the mother of Jesus and Mary Magdalene, so why don't we have more of her words and actions? Why was Aaron Moses' mouthpiece to King Pharaoh, not Miriam? She's listed by the prophet Micah with Aaron and Moses as one who brought the people out of Egypt, yet she's relegated to a side role.

The whole story is ahistorical: there is zero archeological evidence of the Israelites being slaves in Egypt in any significant number; neither is there evidence for the plagues and their subsequent wandering, despite many attempts over the centuries to find it. The promise of the Promised Land was less about historicity or conquest and more about having a home to go to. Many scholars speak of this saga as a political tool and a spiritual life raft. It was written and revised around the time of the Babylonian Exile, starting in 586 BCE, when the people of Israel had been ripped from their homes, their land taken from them, and the Temple—sort of tabernacle 2.0 and God's actual house—destroyed. A story about bondage and liberation, a story about homelessness and wandering and the promise that there was a place at the end where they could lay down their burdens: that resonated in their souls. God was with them, even when they complained mightily. God saved them and fed them. God cared about the daily mundanity of their lives and promised them something better in the future. God ended their oppression by ending the oppressors. That's what the Exodus is about.

And Miriam was there with them too. She celebrated their liberation at the edge of the Reed Sea, she used her voice to push back on injustice, she brought the people water to slake their thirst. Miriam was like Deborah, the wife of ferocity; she was like Zipporah and her mysterious, earthy magic. She was a leader in her own right, whether we remember her whole story or not. We can blame patriarchy for our partial forgetting, and we wouldn't be wrong: we have centuries of examples of men in power erasing women's accomplishments from the narrative and of women flouting that power, going after what they wanted. Because women have led armies and businesses, invented science fiction, and painted images that make you catch your breath. Women invented spread spectrum technology, did the math that actually put men on the moon, and developed a safe, effective cesarean section long before the 1800s. Sometimes we're quiet about it, and sometimes we're like a clap of thunder. You might well ask, Where was Sarah Breedlove or Mary Shelley or Artemisia Gentileschi or Hedy Lamarr or Katherine Johnson? Where was Miriam? Here, doing the things that bring them to life.

And God is here, too, cheering us on in our Exodus. God is not absent from the narrative; God has not given a stamp of approval on our misery. God is with us even when we complain mightily; God saves and feeds and cares about the mundanity of our lives. God liberates us from the captivity of abuse and loneliness and racism and misogyny. Weeping endures the night, the psalmist wrote, but joy comes in the morning. And like the light of a clear, blue morning, the Promised Land isn't just far off; it's already here. Perhaps in bits and pieces, perhaps hard to see, but here.

Where is Miriam? She is here, right here, in you.

5

Delilah

We Don't Need Another Hero

> How can you say, "I love you," when your heart is not
> with me?
>
> —JUDGES 16:15

D o you remember that novel *Jude the Obscure* by Thomas Hardy? It's a corker, let me tell you: it starts off depressing and difficult and gets steadily worse. And just when you think it can't possibly get more miserable for our hero, that it couldn't be more wretched and dismal, it does. Judges is exactly like this, with Israel in the place of the titular Jude and with somewhat less Victorian language, depending on your translation.

Judges is a lot to take in: it has some really epic stories laced with increasingly horrifying violence, women with surprising amounts of agency, men who seem to be focused only on what brings them pleasure, precious little caring for anyone, really, and all organized around the rule of a series of judges. They aren't what you're picturing, though: they didn't wear black robes or carry a ceremonial gavel, and they weren't lawyers or even particularly wise. The judges of Israel didn't so much adjudicate as make war. After the Moses-and-Miriam Exodus era and just before the era of kings came the judges, kind of like interim CEOs who slowly bled the company dry rather than helping it become stable. Really, they were more like warlords than anything. Sometimes they were pretty ok at their jobs—Deborah wasn't too bad in the wisdom department—but mostly their jobs consisted of killing a bunch of humans. The Israelites, you see, had finally arrived in the Promised Land full of excitement and spring garden plans but then realized the land flowed with neither milk nor honey. And, if you can believe it, there were already people living there, and further, they were obliged to kill them all. Some promise.

The judges were the people's response to this mess. They were meant to deliver the people from the "oppression" of the Canaanites and the Jebusites and the Hivites and all the other folk living in the land. The Israelites, of course, were the heroes of this whole narrative and God's best beloved, and while they constantly screwed up, their violence was written as objectively better than the Canaanites'. Scripture speaks of these other people as foreign nations, filthy and sinful, though of course it's Israel who has invaded and started killing willy-nilly. Similarly, colonizers and invaders treated native peoples across the world as expendable roadblocks to "civilization" and discovery. The judges led raids and battles against these "foreign" folk and killed them in droves. All in the name of keeping Israel pure and free from temptation. Which didn't work at all.

The narrators of this and other books in the Hebrew Bible want us to understand that Israel's failure then to murder every last person who was already in the Promised Land is why, in the short term, they go from triumphant pilgrims to disgusting, violent losers at the end of Judges. And, more importantly, why, centuries later, they were far from home, prisoners of war in Babylon mourning and asking themselves, What did we do to deserve this? It's a lot to take in, I know, but basically, the pivotal historical and theological moment for Israel was when they were invaded by Babylon in 586 BCE. Most if not all of the Hebrew scriptures need to be seen as a response, an attempt to make sense of this massive, horrific event. This is not revisionist history but is literally in the text of Judges: Israel was invaded and mutilated because the people fell in love with the gods of the people they didn't massacre. Perhaps you've found yourself in a similar predicament—likely not being captive in Babylon, but what do I know—and you staggered around your own mind wondering what you did that brought such suffering. Maybe you can pinpoint something you did; maybe you find another scapegoat to blame your troubles on, like immigrants or political correctness or late-stage capitalism. The thing is—well, we'll get to the thing later.

Somewhere in the middle of this mess in Canaan, when things were definitely not going well but were not yet at their worst, there was a guy called Samson. He had a miraculous birth and was dedicated to God's service as a Nazirite—a particular religious sect where they didn't drink booze or cut their hair. He was tall and strong, a picture of muscley masculinity. All well and good so far. Samson was a man of huge appetites—for food, for women, for violence. He comes across as a cartoon strongman, biceps bulging, able to leap tall buildings in a single bound, temper ready to explode with comedic, red-faced anger. He was a man's man, the hero we deserve in these trying times. If you've ever seen those truly awful paintings of superbuff Jesus flexing and breaking the cross into pieces—yes, this is a real thing—Samson looked like that. He was strong, but it was for the Lord, y'all—give it up for Samson the Nazirite!

By the time it was Samson's turn to be a judge in Israel, the Philistines were the enemy du jour, and his role as a judge was questionable at best. The book itself describes what a judge was meant to be like, but somehow Samson didn't fit into it at all. He was more like a folktale strongman and a cautionary tale. But what was he cautioning us against? His great triumph at the end was vengeance for losing his eyes, not justice for the people. And Delilah supposedly represents all women's dangerous allure but she bore little fault for anything that happened in the story. By anyone's standards, Samson was not much of a judge. We are meant to see him, I think, as a fallen hero, a man shaped by the lawlessness of his time and, of course, the evil, evil Canaanites. So his being an ass is not only textual—it's expected.

Before we get to Delilah, let me tell you just a little of Samson's history so that you can fully appreciate her response to him. Immediately before we meet Delilah, we are told that Samson had a dalliance with a prostitute. There is no judgment in the text for this action, and this little episode is more to demonstrate his ridiculously great strength when he lifted up the entire city gate and carried it at a run to a nearby city for reasons he did not vouchsafe to anyone. Before that, he was married to another Philistine woman. The text actually says that even though this was a bad idea and socially unacceptable, it was God's will so that there would be a pretext to destroy the Philistines. Weird. Then follows some excessively violent one-upmanship: at the wedding feast, Samson's in-laws were angered by his toast, so he killed thirty of his new family and ran off; they remarried the wife to the best man, so Samson burned all their crops; they killed the wife and her dad, so Samson killed the rest of them; the Israelites tried to turn him in, so he killed a thousand people. Heroic, am I right?

Enter Delilah. I'd be willing to wager dozens of dollars that you have a story about her in your head that isn't true. Something about her being sexually aggressive, manipulative, and vile; about her being the villain in Samson's heroic story; and about poor, honest Samson being taken in by her lies, yes? Delilah, the painted lady, the downfall of good, honest men! But of course she's not. Or she's not that particular brand of evil, anyway.

We only know a few things about her. Delilah's name might mean "flirtatious" or, by one account, "she who makes weak," though I'm inclined to think that's a retcon. We know she was from a town called Sorek, near Jerusalem, but the text is completely uncommunicative about her nationality. And we know that Samson loved her. We don't know if they were married, what her job was, or whether she loved him back, only that Samson loved this woman Delilah from Sorek. And immediately after that, we learn that she was invited by the Philistine government—"the lords of the Philistines," it says—to find this big, strong thorn in their side's weakness and to be paid handsomely for it.

And Delilah did it. She went to Samson and asked, direct as you please, "Won't you tell me what makes you weak?" Samson said, "Sure, little lady. The only thing that could contain these muscles is a bunch of those fresh bowstrings they have down at the market. The ones made from tendons, you know? Yup, those sure would put me in a bind." Then maybe he winked dramatically at her. (I like to imagine that he thought his punning was pretty clever.) So she found that precise make and model of bowstring down at Ye Olde Sporting Goodes, tied him up, and then yelled for the Philistine soldiers who were hiding in her closet. But of course he broke those bonds immediately, because he lied.

So again she asked, "Please won't you tell me what makes you weak?" and again he lied. He said, "Sure thing, darlin'. The only thing that could tucker me out is some brand-new ropes, never been used." (I like to think she looked at him with narrowed eyes, assessing whether he was messing with her again.) So she picked up some brand-new, still-in-the-box ropes she had lying around, tied him up, and again yelled for the Philistine soldiers hiding in her closet. But Samson broke those ropes as well.

A third time she asked him, "Quit playing, man, how do I make you weak?" And a third time he lied. He said, "Of course, sweetheart. Just weave my hair into your loom where you're weaving up that neat rug you showed me the other day. Couldn't possibly pull loose from that, could I?" (One begins to wonder if Samson was a little kinky and felt uncomfortable actually asking for what he wanted.) So when he fell asleep, she did just that and called yet again to the Philistine soldiers hiding in her closet, now quite used to chilling in there with her clothes and cedar blocks. But Samson woke and pulled his hair free from her weaving and laughed.

I feel it's important to notice that Delilah has been nothing but up front with Samson to this point. She has not lied to him once, she has not used anything remotely resembling "wiles" to convince him of anything, and Samson himself has lied to her at every turn. It's true that she's conspiring to have him arrested, which is maybe not great, but she's not making a secret of it at all—three times Samson has lied to her and then seen her call soldiers hidden in her own damn house. What in the world is he thinking?

Delilah tried one more time. The lure of the money must have been strong, or she was seeing Samson more clearly after all this time together and she was ready to be truly rid of him. The text says she "nagged" or "tormented" him until he finally gave in, which is unfair, as women are accused of these things simply because we have an opinion. She asked him, "How can you say, 'I love you,' when your heart is not with me?" So he told her one last ridiculous story about how his strength was really in his hair because he's never had it cut, on account of being a Nazirite and dedicated to God. Such a righteous, pious man, as we've seen. Only this time, he was telling the truth, and apparently, she could tell. Delilah convinced the Philistine government to give her the money in advance, and she went back to her house to lull her big, dumb Samson to sleep. "Dumb," really? Yes. Did he think she wouldn't call the soldiers this time? Or that his giant muscles would save him? Or that it had all been a little violent foreplay like Morticia and Gomez Addams?

One of the Philistines shaved off Samson's hair while he slept curled up around Delilah's knees. Some commenters say she drugged him this time around, though the text doesn't say that, and he hadn't shown himself as one who would need convincing to sleep. He woke to Delilah's now familiar shout to the men in the closet and thought to jump up and take them all, maybe forgetting that he'd told her the actual truth, maybe regretting his swagger? They captured him, gouged out his eyes, and carted him off to prison, where he was forced into labor and made to dance for the amusement of the Philistine lords and ladies. The word *ignominious* comes to mind. In the end, his hair began to grow back, giving him enough strength to push on the load-bearing columns and collapse it on himself and the three thousand people inside. Even in death, Samson's actions were not heroic: he himself said it was vengeance for losing his sight—for himself alone, not for anything the Philistines had done to his people.

And where did Delilah end up? The narrator doesn't much care, since she's served her purpose to bring Samson down. It was her desire that moved things along, her action at the center of the story. I hope the exorbitant sum she was paid by the Philistine government was a sweet nest egg for her or that it at least provided her some security in a world not designed for women's independence. No, she disappeared from the narrative as soon as she called the soldiers in. Samson went on to imprisonment, humiliation, and death; Delilah to the dregs of history. But why? Is it truly because she was so unredeemable or scheming? How was she worse than, say, Jacob or David or Abraham? Or even God themself in the book of Ezekiel?

Let's be clear: it's because she was a woman, and men fear the power women have over them. Maybe not every man—perhaps you, dear male reader, are not like those other men who fear being betrayed, being made fools of, being made weak. Congratulations. Over the years and across cultures, how many women have been accused of witchcraft or of unfaithfulness and then were maimed or murdered? How many women's scientific or artistic achievements have been claimed by men because the women couldn't possibly have understood? Consider how the male characters in Bram Stoker's *Dracula*, even though it is fiction, respond to Mina Murray, the only person who actually knows what's going on: they brush aside her information and send her off by herself while the men work out what to do. Murray is clever and resourceful, but how could she possibly know more than they, learned men meant to protect delicate young women? Mary Magdalene was called a prostitute for centuries because the male-led church couldn't stomach a woman with money and opinions taking a leading role with Jesus. Eve was blamed for the downfall of all humanity and very quickly became a metaphor for the evil within every woman. The very presence of a woman is seen as both a threat and a sexual invitation. Thus Delilah became synonymous with sexual betrayal.

Only, the betrayal Samson experienced was self-inflicted. The foolishness, the being made weak—that was all his. Delilah did exactly what she said she'd do. And this particular story, along with countless others, has been a cautionary tale for centuries: don't trust women, particularly women you're intimate with, because they're all deceitful at heart; they're all out to get you. Isn't that what Ahasuerus thought about Vashti's unwillingness to parade herself before him? (Spoilers: yes. See chapter 12.)

I know some of y'all are reading this and thinking, *Sure, she was up front, but she was up front about helping him get killed. She did literally sell him out. That's not something a good person would do.* Fair enough, she's not a hero, but I'm not convinced she's straight-up evil because she stood up to a bully of a man, you know? Delilah was not playing a game here—her life could very well have been in danger. I don't need to redeem her in some way so that she's palatable for conversations over afternoon tea or for an embroidery sampler. Not every woman in scripture, or in the world, has been hard done by and is in need of refurbishment. Perhaps she was a prostitute, though that doesn't mean she was a horrible sinner—the world's oldest profession is old because women have used what they had to survive for longer than we had a way to judge it. Perhaps she was his wife, though that doesn't mean she loved him at all or had any say in the union. Perhaps she was a Philistine agent, angry at these Israelite invaders, ready to take her own revenge. She doesn't need to be a hero any more than Samson needs to be. They are both broken people living in a broken world.

In the global COVID-19 pandemic, we hear a lot of talk about heroes. There are yard signs, bake sales, cute viral videos of medical professionals dancing or their families and friends being silly to support them as well as heartbreaking stories of nurses and doctors pleading with people to stay home and wear masks. In the fall of 2020, the attention turned to teachers and their heroism—they put in so much hard work to educate our kids, to make this time fun and engaging—and it's all true! These people are risking their lives and working extremely hard. And so are waiters and grocery store clerks and mail carriers. Aren't they heroes too, especially when they have to deal with our entitled bullshit about not wearing masks?

Much of the narrative about heroes in the United States revolves around law enforcement, and our Black and Native and Latinx siblings have been crying out for centuries that badges do not confer heroism. Of course there are good and kind people who become police officers; of course there are people wanting to make a difference, but the system itself is altogether flawed. Slavery is still enshrined in the Thirteenth Amendment to our Constitution and active in our prisons and jails. No matter how well-intentioned, which itself is debatable, our criminal justice system is not a heroic example of order triumphing over chaos but a sign of our similarity to the Israelites of long ago. Executing people on the street or in their cars without due process is not heroic. The greed that created the concept of a racial hierarchy is with us still, undiminished. Our problems weren't solved by Abraham Lincoln or Martin Luther King Jr. or Barack Obama, nor were they solved by Moses or Miriam or the judges. We are not heroes for no longer buying and selling Black bodies. Nor are we villains pure and simple when we've grown up in a system that privileges white over Black. We can lean one way or another, to be sure, whether we mean to or not.

We think of heroes as perfect, even their imperfections worthy of emulation. In our minds, heroes become right and righteous and unquestionable. But that's too easy. Dorothy Day, the selfless human who created the Catholic Worker Movement, famously said, "Don't call me a saint, I don't want to be dismissed that easily." The same is true for villains: laying blame for our troubles at a single person's feet is dishonest. It's not just Samson who's abandoned God and the ways of justice and peace; it's all the people. It's not just Delilah working this gig to save herself; it's all of us.

Our leaders are only representatives of we the people, sometimes cartoonish representations of what we're already doing. We are where the rot is and where the grace is.

My point is, we can become unquestionable heroes in our own minds, we can lend perfection to our culture or our job or the stories we tell ourselves, and we can lay blame for all our troubles at the feet of whomever is convenient and vulnerable enough not to fight back, but these are all lies. Calling Samson a hero and Delilah a villain, and vice versa, is a lie. Delilah isn't a hero, but neither is Samson, and neither are we in the way we think of them. If being a hero is what we are called to, we are all failing.

But that's not our call. We are all turning our backs on God in one way or another in favor of making ourselves comfortable. COVID-19 and systemic racism and climate change and all the rest: this is our Thunderdome. We don't need yet another epic battle with clear heroes and villains. We need to see that there's life beyond wherever we find ourselves, there is a possibility for something better that we can grasp with both hands like Delilah. We need a way home like the Israelites in Exile did. Maybe that way home is in standing up to bullies and in honestly naming what we need and what we'll be taking.

6

The Levite's Concubine

It Gets Better. Eventually.

> "Get up," he said to her, "we are going." But there was no answer.
>
> —JUDGES 19:28

It gets better, they say. Miserable now? Sick or afraid or pissed the hell off? It'll end. I one-hundred-percent believe this to be true. Sometimes, though, it gets infinitely worse first.

Judges, as a whole, is pretty rough. The people known as the Hebrews or the Israelites made it to the Promised Land of Canaan, and the milk and honey they were promised didn't so much flow as dry up like blood from a wound, leaving a crusty mess. It was a fertile place, to be sure: figs and garlic and grapes and olives and wheat grew with abandon. Goats and sheep grazed scenically on the mountains. Probably there were bees too. But it turns out the land already had people living in it, so obviously, the newly arrived Israelites went about murdering them by the thousands to legitimize their own claim to it. Things went from charmingly bad (Jael killing Sisera by nailing his head to the ground) to execrable (the story you're about to read). In the beginning, women had a voice and were listened to, but slowly their words and their agency were stripped away. Men began with strength and a modicum of compassion, but their strength became posturing and their compassion cruelty.

The judges themselves were tribal leaders meant to be wise deliverers, but on the ground they were a lot messier and the text itself looks disapprovingly at them. Here at the end of Judges where this story picks up, there was no king in Israel and every man did what was right in his own eyes—not the generic *man* often used for "everyone" but *ish*, "male person." Even the Levites, the descendants of Moses and Miriam's brother Aaron, the ones who were called to minister in the tabernacle and be in the very presence of God, were walking disasters.

This chapter should come with some trigger warnings, I'm afraid. It is profoundly violent and disturbing, and it includes sexual content, adult language, and peril—so damn much unnecessary peril it makes me sick. So if you'd like to skip it, I won't criticize.

This particular walking disaster of a Levite from the backwater hills of Ephram, he took a wife. Or concubine. Slave? She's definitely more than just a lover or a servant, but given the story, she's somewhat less than a wife. It's unclear, though, because she is the object of his verb—he takes her as his own. A common enough grammatical construction, but the history of gender and marriage suggests that single word is chock full of meaning. You're going to read into that relationship different things depending on your own gender, your own experience. Men are unlikely to notice the grammar simply because it is common and they are the beneficiaries. Women are likely to look at each other over the top of the book and communicate with their eyes, *Typical*. Perhaps it is an innocent phrase; perhaps it isn't. Either way, at this point in history, she was property, with no story of her own, no property of her own, and here, no voice of her own.

Something happened between them—either she cuckolded him or she got angry with him—yet again it's not clear grammatically, and so the offended party isn't clear either. Had he done something to hurt her that caused her anger or her infidelity? Had she been selfish or overly sensitive and hurt him? The particular moment is uncertain, but as the story progresses, we are shown it could only be his honor, his property, that was at stake. Whatever it is that happened, it's bad enough that she left him—one of her only two actions in the story—and returned to her father.

The Levite was so upset by this, so miserable on his own, so ashamed of his behavior, and so desirous of doing the good, hard work of relationship that he waited four whole months before going after her. He said he wanted to "speak to her heart," which sounds lovely and tender, but that's the last we hear of it. His running after his wife-slash-concubine might seem like a romantic gesture, the climax of a big summer movie, but did he really seek reconciliation, or was it lip service? The phrase he used, "to speak to her heart," is a phrase that also shows up in Genesis after Shechem raped Dinah and later in Hosea when God wooed their lover Israel back after leaving her with nothing at the mercy of violent lovers. It comes across as disingenuous. Once the Levite finally arrived at the wife-slash-concubine's father's house, all that happened was days upon days of male bonding: "No, no, stay! Have another beer! The game's about to come on. You don't want to leave yet." There was no conversation with the wife-slash-concubine, no reference made to her at all. The Levite spoke to her dad's heart, not to hers.

When they did finally leave together, they stopped overnight along the way—but not in the big city of Jerusalem where they might have had a safer, more cosmopolitan experience. Jerusalem was currently in the hands of non-Israelites who couldn't be depended upon to offer hospitality. No, they pressed on to scenic Gibeah, a town of good, wholesome Benjaminites, who, it turns out, were awful, depraved Benjaminites. The wife-slash-concubine, of course, was not consulted at all. How could she possibly have had anything to say about the decision?

Anyway, in Gibeah, the Levite and the wife-slash-concubine found shelter with an old man who was actually from back their way in Ephram. This is presented as glorious luck, though it is immediately undercut by his wheedling wealth and promises from them in exchange for his hospitality. Perhaps not as hospitable as one might hope. Then follows a story you might find familiar: the men of the town came banging on the old man's door demanding he send out his guest so that they might know him. Not *know* as in "shake hands cordially and pass the time of day" but "have sex with," and not a tender, Sarah McLachlan lovemaking but "rape for sport." Remember a similar story in Genesis about Lot and some angels in Sodom? Neither of these stories is about homosexuality, you'll notice, but about physical violence and the betrayal of safety for travelers. So, of course, the old man said, "Gentlemen, do not do this vile thing. It's gross. What's wrong with you? He's under my protection, guys; that's sacred. But, you know, my virgin daughter is here. Oh, and my guest's wife-slash-concubine too—want them instead?" The men didn't really care who they got, and the Levite ended up shoving his own wife-slash-concubine out the door and locked it behind her. What was that again about "speaking to her heart"?

And then, well, if it weren't disgusting yet, here is where you might want to look away.

The men of the town—all of them, apparently, not just two or three—raped and tortured her all night. The narrator is terse about the hours and hours of misery she experienced. I suppose it's a blessing that it doesn't go into more detail, and yet in those few words are worlds of pain. This is enough to be getting on with, really, and then it gets worse.

She was trapped in a world of men. What could she possibly do except stagger—maybe crawl—back to the only possible safe harbor, her husband, who threw her at the mob to save himself? She collapsed in exhaustion with her hands on the doorstep and lay there until morning, the hours passing in a haze of pain and questions. The Levite—who you might reasonably expect to have slept poorly at least, who you might hope would rush to the door in the morning to see what had become of her, to collapse in shame and regret, to lift her hands delicately and kiss her fingers, to speak to her heart, to beg God to heal her—was instead impatient to get back on the road. Unconcerned for how she passed her evening, he looked down and said, "Get up, we're going." She didn't answer—was she alive? Was she dead? Of the two primary versions of this story we have in existence, the Hebrew text says nothing; the Greek says she was already dead. And then it gets worse.

He put her on his donkey and headed home, where he picked up the Knife—commentators are very clear about this, *the* knife, not *a* knife, the exact phrasing used when Abraham was about to sacrifice his only son Isaac—he picked up the Knife and dismembered her. You read that right: as calm as can be, considering that only days before he was going to speak to her heart, he chopped her up into twelve pieces to send to all twelve tribes of Israel as a judgment on the men of Benjamin for doing this *to him*. She was treated as a sacrificial animal at this point, the ram caught in the thicket, and it's not even clear when she actually died. Was she dead on his doorstep and that's why she didn't respond? Or was he so disgusted by her when he saw her there, barely breathing, tears and snot and blood and dirt streaked on her skin, that he decided to finish her off himself? Later on, after he'd sent her body parts Priority Mail, he said the people raped her until she died, but that's not what the text says. Neither answer is good, but his interpretation of events seemed to be that it was his property, his honor, his life, that was being threatened. She was only an object, a possession that made him look bad because of its use. And then it gets worse.

The Hebrew Scripture says that all of Israel (*men*, the grammar tells us) responded, "How horrible, nothing like this has ever happened." Meaning her torture and rape? Unlikely. Meaning shipped body parts? Perhaps, but is that really all they were seeing? Meaning a man's honor so insulted and property damaged? Not clear, but the Hebrew Scripture includes an odd feminine grammatical construction: it's possible to translate the men's response as "All who saw *her* said nothing like *her* had never happened before." A weird thing to say, I grant you, and awkwardly phrased, but possibly a tiny moment of awareness of her and her pain. Lots of people say that means nothing: if a chair in French is a feminine word, it doesn't have any bearing on the chair or people's assumptions about chairs and femininity. However, Hebrew uses the masculine to speak about universals and specifically to male people much of the time, and this moment is grammatically different. Maybe you don't care about grammatical distinctions (oh, but it's fascinating, friend! I've got a whole rant about the theology of prepositions), but this one is important because right after it is the phrase "direct your heart to her." Not "consider it with your big brains, take it under advisement, intellectualize and make rational" but "direct your heart" and "to her." This moment points to her as a human in a way the rest of the story refuses to. And, of course, then it gets worse.

Every last man in Israel was shocked—shocked, I tell you. What is the world coming to? So they went to war against the tribe of Benjamin. They absolutely annihilated this tribe of their brothers, leaving a tiny remnant of six hundred men alive. And yes, only men survived because, in their bloodlust, the men of Israel murdered not only soldiers but also every single woman and child. All because of this one Levite and his wife-slash-concubine. And then it gets worse.

Now, because the Israelites were men of honor—I guess we are supposed to believe what they say, not what they do—they could not break the vows they'd made not to let any tribe of Israel die out or to allow their own daughters to marry anyone from Benjamin because of what they did to the Levite. How to solve this conundrum? First, they cried out to God about how hard it was on them to have killed so many of their kinspeople: "How could this vile thing have happened? Mistakes were made!" This legalistic avoidance of compassion is a common response to being caught in wrongdoing, to realizing one's own mistakes. "I'm sorry you felt hurt." "I was just doing my job." "She was asking for it." The men followed up their self-absolution with the logical thing and slaughtered the men of yet another town, Jabesh-Gilead, so that the virgins of that town could be the war brides of the remnant of Benjamin. You know war brides, known for their freely given consent and delight in being raped. Anyway, then it gets worse yet again.

Turns out there were only four hundred women there in Jabesh-Gilead, so the men of Israel "had compassion on the tribe of Benjamin" and allowed them to sneak into neighboring Shiloh and abduct another two hundred women who were dancing at a religious festival to be their wives. How honorable and compassionate. Really speaks to the heart, doesn't it?

That's the end of it getting worse—for now, anyway. Rather like the story of Miriam, you're probably asking, "Where the hell is God?" During all this atrocity, where was the God of Abraham and Sarah, Isaac and Rebekah, Jacob and Rachel and Leah? There was, the narrator hastens to remind us, no king in Israel, and every man (*ish*, again) did what was right in his own eyes. Not God's fault, then? Or just an excuse for shitty behavior? Is a king that much of a magical talisman that the people all do justice and love kindness when they've got one? I'll invite you to look into King David and King Saul and the exhaustive lists of terrible kings in the books of Kings. Look into Henry VIII of England or presidents like Paul Kagame and Juvénal Habyarimana of Rwanda or any leader you'd like. It's almost like a regime change doesn't actually change anything if you're not willing to do the work on yourself, individually and collectively. And it's not like things were sunshine and roses at the beginning of Judges either, but they were a damn sight better than this. With the story of the wife-slash-concubine, Israel had fallen much, much farther than Eve.

So what's the moral of this story? What are we supposed to come away with? And regardless of authorial intent, what are we actually taking away?

I tell you what—I come away with even more disgust at the way men have run the world for centuries. Yes, I know, #notallmen, but also #toomanymen and certainly #menwrotehistory. I guarantee you the women in this story had lots of thoughts and feelings about what was happening around them, whether or not they approved of the patriarchal system they found themselves in. Why don't we hear a single word from any of them? Why is a woman's body a thing and not an embodied soul, created good by God in the beginning? Why is a man's honor—that he seems wealthy and upright regardless of whether he actually is—more important than another person's life, male or female, insider or outsider?

Some people say this story is about God's mercy in keeping the tribes from entirely destroying each other. I suppose God is always doing a new thing with the horror we perpetrate on each other, as Isaiah says in the midst of his own difficult time: "Now it springs up; do you not perceive it?" (Isaiah 43:19 NIV). In this case, no I damn well do not. That the tribe of Benjamin isn't extinct is not enough good news to me, nor any good news considering what they did in retaliation. Why is this story ok to have kept in Holy Scripture?

I'm not advocating for taking it out—that would indeed be revising history, and we need to remember stories like this because they still happen. Women the world over are considered less than men when it comes to pay and hiring and promotion, when it comes to choosing their own spouses, when it comes to having a say about what happens to their bodies. Women the world over are told by men in authority—fathers, brothers, administrators, and politicians—that they can't possibly have the understanding needed to run a corporation or government or even make their own medical decisions. And it's not limited to women: gender nonconforming folk are raped and murdered in alarming numbers every year, most often because some man couldn't handle the discomfort he felt in being attracted to them. Somehow he felt his honor was impugned because this person simply existed. These are stories we need to tell each other because they're not myths—they're real. And we can't change the narrative if we don't know what it is.

Some interpreters say the entire book of Judges is a political condemnation of Saul, the first king of Israel, descended from the tribe of Benjamin, or it's the result of infighting among groups of Levites, or it's a polemic against the Northern Kingdom, blamed for all the troubles that followed. I'm very much a fan of the historical and political reading of scripture—there's so much meat there—but at what cost? That is, do we pay for intellectual, logical readings of stories like this with the painful truth of the vulnerable? Do we end up justifying the violence as part of the big picture and ignoring the people who bore the brunt of the big picture? Judges most definitely traces the struggles of the people of Israel after they arrived in the Promised Land. They themselves made promises to God that they didn't keep. Their decline continues in the books following, but this story? It's about more than a historical through line.

This book and this story in particular are a call to transformation. Look at your lives, look at your choices. For shame! We are clearly not meant to take this Israel as a role model. Here outsiders to the people of the Promise are actually better at practicing hospitality than Israel; they display more virtuous behavior than God's own people. Even now I hear committed church people say with wonder, "You know, my neighbor is an atheist and he's just the kindest, most generous person," as though it's such a surprise that nonreligious folk could have a basis for humanity. But this is precisely the question: No matter what system of belief or unbelief we claim, how are we treating those we consider unworthy? What do we consider them unworthy of in the first place? What does it suggest about us?

Bible scholar Phyllis Trible says our task is to walk alongside the wife-slash-concubine, to be her companion. Walking with her does not justify her pain or even take it away but acknowledges it, bears it with her, shows her and every other person who has been broken by power that they are not alone and that there is something beyond this moment. My pastor friend Alex says, "The worst thing that happens to you is not the last thing that happens to you." In the Hebrew ordering of the books of the Bible, the story of Hannah in 1 Samuel follows this one, and in the Greek ordering, Ruth follows. Hannah and Ruth, women who knew themselves and God deeply, who took control of their lives and shared themselves with others. Hannah and Ruth are companions to this wife-slash-concubine, to this woman who is her own person, even if her story removes her agency.

And there is an empty place in this story, a dotted-line cutout in the shape of us, the reader. Where are we in this story? Where are we when this story is reenacted now? When she and so many other women are betrayed into the hands of sinners?

We offer safe harbor for women who need nonjudgmental medical care at Planned Parenthood. We demand accountability for police departments to reject applicants with domestic violence records. We support women's shelters and group-living organizations so there are places for them to go when they need to get out. We speak up at work and school for the dignity of our trans siblings and advocate for their rights in the medical and judicial systems. We speak up for the outsiders in our communities, immigrants, homeless, and mentally ill where they don't have a voice. We speak up because God gave us voices to make things better today than they were yesterday.

We speak up.

7

Hannah

I Put My Thing Down, Flip It, and Reverse It

> Those who were full have hired themselves out for bread,
> but those who were hungry are fat with spoil.
> The barren has borne seven,
> but she who has many children is forlorn.
>
> —1 SAMUEL 2:5

My father used to say, when he was telling us stories about the world before we were born, "That was before you were a gleam in your mother's eye." As a child, I was fascinated that there was a time before me. As a teenager, less so—my parents looked at each other with lust? Gross. As an adult, I get it. Believe it or not, there was a time before you existed, kid.

Before the prophet Samuel had his big moments telling the priest Eli that God knew all about his sons' poor life choices, before anointing the very first king of Israel, he was a gleam in his mother's eye. Back then, our heroine Hannah, whose name means "beautiful" and "charming," was in love with Elkanah and he with her. She was feisty and stubborn and a talented poet. He was more patient and caring than she'd expected in a husband. They were young and in love and, though things were hard in Israel, they made a life together. But no matter how much their eyes gleamed when they looked at each other, no matter how much they tried and enjoyed the trying, they could not conceive. Or, rather, in the parlance of the time, Hannah could not conceive—God did not open her womb.

Infertility is no small thing. In Hannah's time, not only were children a signal of a woman's worth as a human being; they were also a built-in retirement plan. Women in particular were dependent on their adult children caring for them when they were too old to care for themselves. Hannah's desire for a child wasn't one-dimensional—it wasn't only about societal worth or fulfilling traditional roles as wife and mother or even about loving and being loved by another person—it was a multilayered thing, for her and for anyone wanting children. She longed for a child and it was impossible, goes the story. She was "barren" like a field that had been planted with pumpkins but which didn't produce a single one, not even a slender vine. I've noted before that men in the Bible are never described as barren or as poor farmers; it is only the woman whose body fails the planting. Unfair. Infertility was an old song, a common enough experience that it was a repeated metaphor for the absence of God's life-giving Spirit.

For years this went on, the two of them becoming increasingly frantic. Sometime along the way, Elkanah came to her, looking apprehensive, and said, "I'm going to take a second wife." Hannah had perhaps been expecting this. It wasn't odd for men who could afford them to have multiple wives, and anyway, he needed to have children to pass on their land and property. Who knows how Hannah felt about the new wife at first—resigned, maybe, but possibly intrigued or even excited to have a sister and friend brightening up the place. But that wasn't to be. Elkanah married Peninnah, whose name means "fertile" or "prolific," a reversal of Hannah's existential situation. Peninnah had childbearing hips that didn't lie. She bore Elkanah several children, and so his need was sated.

But Hannah—beautiful, charming, stubborn, gleaming Hannah—was empty. Her husband loved her regardless, but what was that worth when she went to the well or the market and people pointed and whispered? And more than that, she longed to hold her own baby, to wash its tiny ears and feel its tiny mouth suck on her finger. She longed to feel for herself what the women around her felt—the driving need to protect, to cradle. And more than that, when she lay on her bed at night next to Elkanah, she stared into the darkness of the rafters, her stomach in knots as she thought about what would happen to her when she was old with no one to care for her. Her tears were the dirge her soul hummed.

Every year the family went up to Shiloh, a bustling city of rich smells, street musicians, and shops full of people. They went up to make a sacrifice at the Temple there where the Ark of God rested, killing animals on the altar as offerings to cleanse their sin, to lift up thanksgivings, to release guilt. The blood of the animals and the smoke from their cooking were meant to be pleasing to God. Honestly, have you ever smelled a good, slow, dry-rub barbecue? That there is proof God loves us. And though it's violent, it makes a kind of sense to offer up the life flowing through our veins to the source of that life. It's not exactly magic, but that we have breath in our lungs and blood in our bodies feels a little magical.

Anyway, every year when Elkanah had offered his sacrifice, he brought back meat from the sanctuary for his family. Legally, he was supposed to give a portion to each person in his family, which meant Peninnah's family would get much more meat than did poor, childless Hannah. But because Elkanah loved her, he gave her extra meat from the sacrifice. Nothing says love like an extra steak, I say. What a caring gesture; what a caring man! Only, Hannah didn't want pity, she didn't want meat, she didn't even want the blood sacrifice—she wanted a baby.

And Peninnah saw. She herself was full of life, her house filled with the songs children sing. She looked at Hannah not with pity but with scorn. The two of them are described as rivals, but they had more than a schoolyard disagreement: the Hebrew word here is used in other places to mean "warring enemies." "You must have done something to deserve God closing your womb," Peninnah would say in the morning before they went to the market. "How sad it must be," she'd say to her friends in the town loudly enough for Hannah to overhear, "to be so empty, to be so unloved and unwanted, even by God." And they'd laugh, not even trying to hide it from her. Hannah held her head high, reminded herself that she was Elkanah's love, that God parted the sea so God could open her womb. Sometimes it worked, but Peninnah was prolific in childbirth and Hannah had lost the gleam in her eye.

Hannah wept. She refused to eat and lay on her bed staring at the wall for hours on end. Elkanah worried for her. He came and sat on the bed at her feet, his hand resting on her ankle, his thumb rubbing little circles. He sat in silence at first, then asked, "Why is your heart sad?" He asked, "Why are you crying and why won't you eat?" And he asked, "Am I not more to you than ten sons?" This man who loved her so, and who enjoyed her intensity, and whose eyes gleamed when he looked upon her, he also just didn't get it. Wasn't he enough for her? I don't know, was she enough for him? Obviously not, with Peninnah in the picture. Wrong question, brother. Hers was a different kind of love, a different need, a different pain altogether. I don't know if Hannah rolled away from him in silence or if she rose up with fire in her eyes to take him to task for his insensitivity, but something changed in her this time. This time, this year, this moment, things would be different.

When they next went to Shiloh to make offerings, she went to the Temple and stood outside it. She looked at the stone stacked so carefully to make the walls and at the woven hangings on either side of the door. She marveled that people could make such things. She despaired that people could be so cruel. And she prayed: silently, eyes closed and looking inward at her pain and at God's presence in the temple of her body. She spoke directly to God, desperate and longing, vowing that if God gave her a son, she'd give him back as a Nazirite, a kind of monk: "God, if you'd only give me a son, Penny would stop being so mean and I could hold my head up in the market. If you'd only give me a son, I could be a mother. I could care for him. If you'd only give me a son, I wouldn't be so lonely. If you'd only give me a son, I wouldn't have to be afraid. If only, if only . . ."

She prayed long and hard and silent, eyes closed, lips moving with her desperation. The priest Eli was sitting on a stool at the entrance to the Temple, people watching, you know. And he saw this woman stop and gaze at the building for a while, then close her eyes and—was she mumbling to herself? For goodness' sake, this woman was drunk here outside God's holy place! He marched over to her, full of certainty and indignation, and said, "Woman, stop making a spectacle of yourself. Go home and sober up!"

Hannah opened her eyes and looked at this little man who couldn't possibly understand her. Hannah opened her mouth and spoke: "I'm not drunk; I am sad. I am praying; I am pouring out my soul like melted wax. Can you not see it written on my face?" She said, "I am filled with anxiety and vexation"—I adore that word; it's so evocative and Victorian—"and I am not worthless." This word *worthless*, *beliyyaal*, was used previously for the rapists at the end of Judges and is used later to describe Eli's own no-good, very bad, priestly sons. What a word to name yourself with or, rather, to unname yourself. She was so troubled, so sad and abused and frustrated and stuck that she felt *beliyyaal*, and she knew, deep in her gut, that it was a lie. Hannah knew she was supposed to be meek and quiet, particularly in the presence of an authority figure like Eli, but her pain, even her anger with God for closing her womb, could not and should not be hidden. Here the song of her soul became a protest song.

The priest Eli, without even knowing what Hannah was praying for but startled and moved by her response, repented of his harsh words and said, "May God grant what you asked." So say we all. And because of her heartfelt prayer, because Eli named her worthiness, "her countenance was sad no longer." It's not that his reversal made everything better but that in asking for what she needed, in saying the thing, she felt liberated, unconstricted. In other words, her shoulder muscles released, her eyebrows softened, her eyes crinkled at the sides, and her face shone like Moses' after speaking with God. She got her groove back.

Immediately after this, scripture says she went home, had a glass of wine with Elkanah, and put on Marvin Gaye's "Let's Get It On." The two of them embraced as the camera faded to black. Hell yeah, Hannah! What it really says is "Elkanah knew his wife," truly in the biblical sense. And then it says, "God remembered her," and she got pregnant.

I have to ask, Did God actively close her womb or just forget about her? Either option is kind of shitty. Did she do something to deserve the intentional closing? Is God really that forgetful? At the time, the sense was that God made all things happen or not happen simply by willing them to. Perhaps this "closed womb" image was simply a helpful shorthand for infertility. Or perhaps it was comforting to know that someone was in control, even if things were hard, that there were intention and organization. There are conspiracy theorists who believe that 5G phone networks are giving us COVID-19 or that aliens killed JFK—they believe these things because, as odd as they sound, they bring order to a chaotic and frightening world. Even if it's not true, to think that the right prayer or the right action might change our situations or change God's mind brings a sense of order in a world where we often feel helpless.

At any rate, after forty weeks of growing a person inside her belly, after the pain and fear of childbirth, Hannah held little baby Samuel in her arms. Perhaps she was too exhausted at first to appreciate his scrunched-up face, as I was when my Abi was born—when the nurse asked me if I wanted to hold her, I said no and fell asleep. Or perhaps she was so relieved that they had both survived the trauma of birth that she laughed and cried at the same time, that after seeing his furry little shoulders she was overcome with love and connection. How could anyone possibly love their child more than she did in that moment? She would be exhausted, of course, but this was her son, her firstborn, her world.

Hannah didn't go to the Temple with Elkanah the next time he went to make sacrifices and probably not for at least a couple of years—before the modern era of formula and baby experts, women regularly breastfed their children until they were three or even older. Perhaps when she was ready to dedicate Samuel to the Temple, it was like sending him off to kindergarten at a boarding school. It must have been painful. He had survived his childhood, never a guarantee at that point in history, and he was her only child, her future, her triumph. She was his only, his best, his mother. My kids are still about a decade from heading off to college, and I already feel lost and empty because of it.

The day Hannah took Samuel to the Temple, she dressed them both in their best clothes, she took her most beautiful bull and some homemade wine, she packed him up a bundle of her most delicious pastries. When they arrived, she stood before Eli, her feet planted on the ground, her heart pounding. She said, "Remember that woman you thought was drunk? I prayed that day for a child and, look, here he is!" I like to imagine Eli looking at her flabbergasted at first but then seeing in her eyes the trust in God that he longed for all of Israel to have. I imagine he nodded, a grin creeping onto his face as he offered little Samuel his hand. And Hannah, what did she do? Did she give him last-minute advice for making friends? Did she hug him and weep? Did she walk away, forcing herself not to look back?

Hannah sang a song. But not just any song: in the playlist of biblical songs, this one is on the greatest hits album. It's a song of gratitude, a song of protest and prophecy, a song of violence, grief, mercy, folly, joy, sex, and redemption. Hannah's Song is a lot like Mary's Song in the book of Luke—many believe Mary's is based on Hannah's. In her lyrics, Hannah sang of the comfortable becoming afflicted and the afflicted finding comfort. She sang about power coming to nothing and those who were considered nothing—the poor, the sick, the oppressed—finding their voices and using them. She sang of life literally coming out of the place of the dead, Sheol. Reversals abound because Hannah knew our God is a God of reversals.

God constantly raises up unexpected people, poor people, young people, enemy people you wouldn't have looked at twice to receive blessing. I mean, honestly, even in working on salvation for the creation, God became a vulnerable, soft, squishy human—it's ridiculous, why not just show yourself in all your godly might? And then that human-God named Jesus literally died to make his point about loving sacrifice—what kind of god does that? The kind of god who is deeply invested in the lives of people who suffer, that's who. Hannah's Song is the old English ballad "The World Turned Upside Down" but with a beat, so you can dance to it.

Scholars are pretty sure this song Hannah sang was written later than the rest of the book because of exciting grammar reasons (simply put, it uses vocabulary that came into vogue later), but that's common throughout the Bible. Pieces were put together because they fit the theological point the writers were making—here, that God sees and hears people who suffer, that God remembers those who feel forgotten, that the pain Israel was feeling in that moment would end eventually. In the long tradition of women singing battle songs, Hannah brought hers to a wild crescendo in the last verse: while a thunderstorm rages around them, God's enemies (and *our* enemies) will fall into confusion and ruin. Take that, Peninnah! Her song is prophetic, not in the sense of telling the future but in the sense of speaking the truth about what the future could be. Hannah, like Mary Theotokos and like mothers the world over, was a prophet, singing possibility into being rather than failure, seeing hope and new life for the world in the eyes of her newborn.

I haven't experienced infertility myself; though I've walked through it with a number of friends and parishioners, I don't pretend to really know how painful it is. They say there's a feeling that their bodies have betrayed them, that there's something wrong with them, that they're not whole people because they can't do this one thing. Those things aren't true, yet they feel so real. Hannah's infertility is part of a long tradition of "barren women" who are miraculously impregnated—it's an easy metaphor for God's power because it feels insurmountable and full of grief and then is spectacularly reversed. Where the land was unproductive and unfruitful, suddenly there is a lush garden. How could we not celebrate such a story? Yet so many people don't find themselves in the happy ending like Hannah—they don't get pregnant; they don't experience that lushness.

Elkanah tried to make it better for her, he really did. He is all of us who are outside of the pain and grief trying to fix it for her. We say, "You can try again" or "At least you've got your health" or, worst of all, after a miscarriage, "God needed another little angel." No, they damn well didn't, and those kinds of phrases only dismiss what the person is feeling. "Aren't I more than ten sons?" Elkanah said, trying desperately to show her how much he cared for her, how much he worried. But it sounds like "You shouldn't be so sad." He meant well, but he was shortsighted. He minimized her pain and her social status because he couldn't really know what she was going through. Of course there is possibility outside of childbirth; of course there's fruitfulness beyond this moment. But this moment is miserable, and because of its misery, it's sacred, set apart. Suffering people need to walk through it, and we need to let them.

Elkanah, shortsighted as he might have been, was a good husband. He might not have responded well to her pain—friends, I don't respond well to my own husband's pain, typically with impatience and anger—but he tried, which is more than can be said for most husbands in scripture who don't even notice their wives' suffering. We don't need to judge him too harshly, since he seems to be naming her value and her humanity outside of childbearing. As the Fresh Prince would say, "He a little confused, but he got the spirit."

There are those who say there is nothing feminist in Hannah's story because she was praying for conventional things—a child, social prestige, and stability. What an unfair assumption—feminism doesn't mean you can't long to be a mother, doesn't mean you have to leave your husband or be a CEO. Feminism simply means being able to make your own choices without being restricted by your gender. Be a firefighter and also wear pink and have ten babies—go wild! If you chose it, do it; if someone else chose it for you, consider how invested you are in it. Hannah chose what she wanted—even if it was colored by societal expectations and safety—and pushed back on the people who said she couldn't. She said with her prayer and her pregnancy and her song, "Stop telling me I'm not supposed to have it or I don't need it or I'm not worthy of it."

Hannah's story is read every year in synagogues at Rosh Hashanah. It's a celebration of a new year, a fresh start. It's the feeling of being forgotten, defeated, and then remembered, put back together. It is the possibility of our own dignity, humanity, and personhood where before we didn't see it. Hannah's voice today is in the mouth of Stacey Abrams, working for every citizen's voice to be heard. Hannah's voice is in the mouth of John Boyega, speaking up for himself and other actors of color. Hannah's voice was in the songs and struggles of Nina Simone. Hannah's voice is in the care of parishioner Beth Townsend teaching children in an underprivileged public school. Hannah's voice is in the mouths of Greta Thunberg and Autumn Peltier and Emma González. Hannah's voice is the voice of every parent who has sent their child off into the world with fear and trembling. Hannah's voice is all around us. Will you join her?

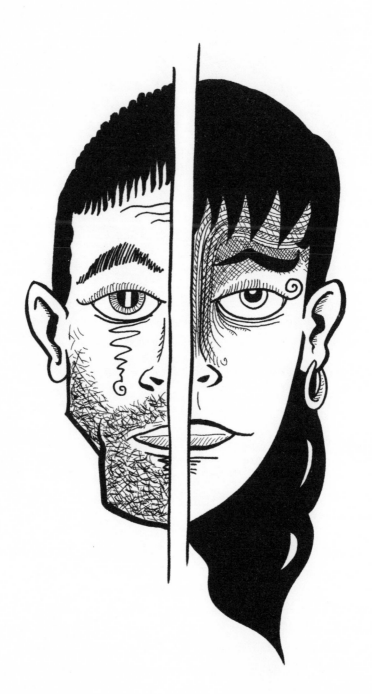

8

Michal and Jonathan

I Have Vague and Messy Positive Feelings toward You

Jonathan loved him as his own soul.

—1 Samuel 18:1

Saul's daughter Michal loved David.

—1 Samuel 18:20

Once upon a time, there were a brother and sister who lived in a palace. Their parents were king and queen, but monarchy was brand spanking new to their country, so it wasn't that fancy a palace yet, more of a big house. I suppose that made them princess and prince, but they didn't care much as children. The brother and sister did everything together. They built forts in the olive orchard, the brother more interested in fortifications and rope ladders, the sister more interested in a place for her art supplies and writing out the rules of their sibling club. They played in the mud, pranked the neighbor kids, and argued about politics with their daddy King Saul.

The brother Jonathan grew up to become a skilled soldier, defeating his enemies in battle and taking on daring raids with

only his closest brothers in arms. His exploits made him the darling of the people and a bit of a showboater—think Dwayne "The
Rock" Johnson in all of his incarnations. One time, the Israelite army had every one of their weapons at the blacksmith for
sharpening—a bit of an oversight there—except for Jonathan's and
Saul's. Jonathan and his armor-bearer snuck off by themselves to
the nearby mountain pass where a Philistine garrison was posted
and killed all twenty men. Another time, King Saul decreed that
all the troops would fast so that God would help them utterly
destroy the Philistines in the next battle. Imprudent, if you ask me
and the narrator—hangry troops wouldn't seem to be the most
effective. Not having heard the decree, Jonathan ate some honey
from a comb he found, then encouraged the troops to pillage the
Philistines' towns for meat. Didn't matter that it was his very own
son, King Saul was ready to have Jonathan killed because of it. But
the people spoke with one voice, as they do in folktales, saying,
"Seriously? He literally just led us to an amazing victory over our
enemies, and you want to kill him for having dinner? God was
with him today!" They wisely didn't add, ". . . and not with you."

Meanwhile, the sister Michal (pronounced "Mee'-chal" with a
guttural "ch" as in *challah*) worked in the palace's garden learning
about herbs and vegetables. She practiced sculpture and embroidery, learned to help women in the palace give birth, and taught
herself calligraphy, upholstery, and small engine repair. Perhaps she
took up prestidigitation. We don't actually know because, as usual,
scripture doesn't care about her interests because they weren't to
do with battle or politics. Still, I imagine she might be played by
someone like a young Angela Bassett, fierce and tender in turns.

One day this guy David showed up in their father's court—
flushed with excitement, his eyes beautiful and soulful, maybe
smelling a little of sheep. Possibly played by Tom Hiddleston, if
for no other reason than his dancing ability. He was a musician
and a shepherd and a war hero, and they'd heard the whispers
that the prophet Samuel had made him the next king. Michal and
Jonathan were intrigued—wasn't Jonathan to be king? Wouldn't

their father Saul be angry about this random shepherd and traveling musician having designs on the throne? Saul was indeed angry but ebbing and flowing, mercurial. He hired David as a harpist to soothe his depression and anger and, it seems, to keep his enemy close. Michal looked at him and loved him. Jonathan, too, looked and loved. Their older sister Merab looked and didn't care one way or the other but found herself betrothed to him.

Michal's love was intense and sudden and inevitable. She is the only woman in scripture said to love a man. Others show their love with epic poetry, with the daily work of relationship, with tolerance. Still others may not have loved their partners at all, not in our modern understanding, anyway. "Michal loved David," it says. How powerful must her love have been for the text to name it so starkly. It is a plot point in the tale being told, important to put her later anger in relief, but I think there's something else here. I think she saw in David a desirable sexual partner, a tender human, and a charismatic leader. I think, in that first moment, she saw all that he could be and longed to be with him on the path to get there.

Jonathan's love was intense and sudden and inevitable. It was in the jubilation of David's triumph over Goliath, with adrenaline still pumping through everyone's veins, that Jonathan watched David speak with Saul, and his heart swelled. The story says, "The soul of Jonathan was bound to the soul of David, and Jonathan loved him as his own soul." The Hebrew here translated as "love" has suggestions of fealty as well as emotion, so many commentators say the love referred to is brotherly and political in nature, not romantic. Perhaps so, but I think there's something else here, something more ambiguous than traditional readings allow. The whole passage and the two men's relationship beyond this moment suggest more. "Soul" is *nephesh*, not just spirit but a person's entire being, their whole self. Jonathan and David's entire selves were bound to each other in emotional loyalty. I think, like Michal, Jonathan saw in David a desirable sexual partner, a tender human, and a charismatic leader. I think, in that first moment, he saw all that he could be and longed to be with him on the path to get there.

So Jonathan approached David and they went some distance away to talk. Jonathan stripped himself almost naked and gave everything he had with him to David—his royal robe and his weapons—to show his vulnerability and loyalty. "Here I am, defenseless, offering myself to you," he said. This was not just a titillating piece of performance art but a covenant, a vow of connection between two people, and, significantly, a transference of power. Because of this, David was successful in every battle Saul sent him to, and he was put in charge of the whole army.

But on the way back home after the fight with Goliath and David and Jonathan's vow, the seed of Saul's jealousy began to sprout again. The women of the nearby towns came out rejoicing and playing instruments and singing war songs. They sang about the thousands Saul had killed and the tens of thousands David had killed, even though, right at that moment, it was just the one Philistine. Saul saw how beloved David was already and grew envious. From that day, Saul watched for ways to have David killed.

As the months went by, Saul would sit on his throne thinking kingly thoughts and see David strumming his harp. He would feel sudden fury looking at his stupid handsome face and his stupid destined-to-be-king hair and would try to kill David with his spear, but David got away. Multiple times Saul sent David off to war, but David just went and won all the time. Saul offered his eldest daughter Merab, the one who wasn't interested, as a reward if David would just go fight some more, thinking he'd die in battle this time for sure, but David said humbly, "Who am I to marry into royalty?" and then won yet again.

Saul was increasingly frustrated that his plots were failing, but then he learned that his younger daughter Michal loved David, and he thought to himself, *This is your chance! Maybe she can be his weak spot, and I can finally be rid of this damn pretender.* So he married Merab off to someone else and had his servants tell David how much he, Saul, admired him, how beloved he was among the people, how he deserved to marry up and cement his relationship with his devoted admirer the king. This scene feels like something from *Downton Abbey* with the servants scurrying between the lords and sharing gossip and everyone manipulating everyone else. David said, "I'm a poor man, y'all; seriously, I literally can't pay her dowry." Was this false modesty meant to earn him more power, or was he actually realistic about his social standing? Saul responded that David could pay the dowry with the currency of one hundred Philistine foreskins. As you do. Again, Saul was expecting David to die in the attempt, all evidence thus far to the contrary, and was startled and probably a bit horrified to see David returning with a bloody bag full of bits of flesh. Just a quick aside: How precise was the surgery David performed? Inquiring minds want to know.

To her great delight, Michal found herself married to the man she loved and longed for. Perhaps she knew about David and Jonathan's covenant, perhaps she didn't mind, perhaps she knew that her relationship would be the only publicly affirmed one, perhaps she stuck out her tongue at Jonathan as she left the wedding on David's arm.

David seemed to be invincible, winning victories left and right, and Saul's plots to do away with him failed, bringing Saul ever more fear and envy. How could this damn upstart be so gifted? How could Saul win back God's favor? He went to his son Jonathan and told him he was trying to kill David, assuming Jonathan would be on board. Jonathan was very much not on board and immediately told David about the danger. He went back to his father and said, "Dad, why in the world are you so angry about David? He's only done good things for you and for us, he's a great soldier, everyone loves him, and even you were excited about his music and his military skills. What gives?" Saul, seeing his error or trying to save face, said, "You are right, my son. I swear I will not kill him." And things were ok for a time.

But again Saul was overcome with rage while David was playing the harp and tried to stab him with a spear. David escaped to his own house and collapsed on the bed, panting and groaning in frustration. Michal bolted the door, closed the curtains, and said, all practicality, "You've got to get out of here. My dad's going to succeed one of these days. We'll make a rope from the bedsheets, and I'll come up with a distraction for tomorrow. Come on then, up and at 'em." Not able to trust anyone around them, she lowered him out of the window herself and created a goat-hair-and-statue dummy to put under the bedsheets like a proto–Ferris Bueller. When Saul sent people to arrest David, she told them he was ill and couldn't possibly be disturbed. Saul demanded that they bring the whole bed up to the palace so he could see for himself and was surprised and livid to find that his own child had chosen her husband over him. She claimed David had threatened her life so she would aid his escape, her lie to Saul probably saving her life.

In the wilderness, David and Jonathan reunited (and it feels so good) and panicked a bit about how bad things had gotten. Could they find a way back to normal? Did Saul know how deeply their connection ran? Was Saul being honest with Jonathan or not? They sat with their backs against a tree, shoulders touching. "Death is only one footstep behind," David said, gazing up at the leaves above. So they made plans to protect him, pretending he'd been called away on family business and arranging for Jonathan to figure out just how Saul was really feeling. They renewed their covenant with many protestations of love and devised a secret method of communication so David would know what had happened.

Saul was again surprised and livid that his own child had chosen his friend and lover over him—so much so that he cursed Jonathan, shaming him for choosing David in words that are painfully reminiscent of allegedly Christian parents rejecting their queer kids. Yes, I know that's reading a modern experience back into ancient words, but also, parents have long had expectations their children didn't live out and have driven them away because of it. Saul's disgust that Jonathan was a "disgrace to your mother's nakedness" suggests he thought their relationship was somehow indecent. Jonathan left the table angry and worried for David's life. He went out early the next day for "archery practice" and took an assistant as cover for his secret communication with David. He shot three arrows into one spot near where David was hiding, the signal that it was indeed him, then shouted to the boy that there was perhaps another arrow beyond, the signal that things were not safe for David. After the boy retrieved the arrows and was dismissed, David and Jonathan kissed and wept and parted ways. (Lest you suspect I'm making this bit up to suit my own narrative, it says right there in 1 Samuel 20, "[David] bowed three times, and they kissed each other, and wept with each other; David wept the more.")

Michal, meanwhile, was back at her house, living her life one day at a time, worrying for her husband and growing increasingly lonely. Would she ever see her David again? Would he come for her? Would they ever live in the palace in peace? And then she heard he'd remarried. Twice. Abigail and Ahinoam. Though polygamy was common for those who could afford to support multiple wives, still Michal felt abandoned. Her own brother had more contact with David than she did, and now there were two more women to take up his time and who were actually with him out there, comforting him, caring for him? And then, betrayal on betrayal, her father sent her off to be married to another man. It should be noted, for a woman to be married to two men simultaneously was incredibly illegal (note the hypocrisy there), but Saul wasn't known for his interest in rules. So Michal was packed off to some guy named Palti.

Eventually, after many more battles and an intriguing interlude with a spiritualist, Jonathan and his brothers were overtaken by the Philistines and killed. Saul was wounded and then took his own life. The Philistines took over Israel and occupied it. And David was heartbroken.

Though Saul had been against him for many moons, he was still something of a father figure to David and a man worthy of respect. He sang a song of lament and praise, of their courage and strength, and then he sang of Jonathan: "Greatly beloved were you to me; / your love to me was wonderful, / passing the love of women." The closest of friends, brothers in arms, of course those manly relationships would be beyond those of mere women. And yet these words speak of a tenderness beyond friendship. I'm certain that Michal grieved her brother, too, though scripture doesn't tell us of it. They had been so similar, so close, once upon a time, and he was gone.

Time passed. The battles shifted away from the Philistines and into fighting between Israel and Judah for the throne Saul had left empty. David grew older and took four more wives, mostly to cement political alliances—Maacah, Haggith, Abital, and Eglah. After all this time, David demanded the return of his first wife Michal, daughter of Saul, probably to legitimate his claim on the throne—Michal, who had been abandoned and ignored, who had been replaced by six wives, who had been sent off to live with another man. And so she was taken away from her second husband Palti like a pawn on a chessboard, and Palti followed after the wagon, weeping as he walked. It's a small detail, but telling. This man, too, loved. Could it be that Michal loved him in return? Could it be that she found some peace with him, that they created a life together, that she'd been ripped from something valuable?

Again, time passed. Again, David took more wives and concubines. He was made king of Israel and united the warring factions. In celebration, he retrieved the Ark of the Covenant, the golden box containing the Torah (that would eventually and quite rightly melt Nazi faces in 1936). He brought it into the new capital Jerusalem with great festivity—everyone around was shouting and singing, playing music and dancing. David himself danced with the people, leaping and spinning like Michael Flatley, wearing only a kind of loincloth sacred to tabernacle worship.

Michal saw him dancing from her window and hated him for it. She hated him for making a fool of himself, she said through gritted teeth later, for breaking the rules of propriety and being naked in front of the sex slaves—did his lust and shame know no bounds? He yelled, "Oh, you think this is shameful? Just you wait, lady—I'll be so embarrassing I won't even be able to look at my own self! Who do you think you are to talk to me that way?!" But the Hebrew text of this story only says she hated him, not that she hated him "for it." His shirtless dance was only the crack in the dam, and Michal had other reasons for her animosity: his abandoning her for Jonathan and then other women, his never giving her a child, his ripping her out of the new life she'd had to make. Her story ends with resentment and childlessness and death.

Michal and Jonathan have no scenes together in this tale, no conversations recorded, no knowing glances across the room saved for posterity. They lived big, messy lives full of intrigue and nation building. They loved fiercely and perhaps foolishly. They were rivals for David's love as David and Saul were rivals for the throne.

There are many who argue that David and Jonathan were definitely not lovers, that the love they shared was a deep bond of friendship, a stellar example of nontoxic masculinity. In the earliest Jewish commentary, their relationship is held up as an example of enduring love because it was unselfish. Not to argue with those rabbis, but I'm not convinced of that argument. The traditional platonic understanding makes sense because both Judaism and Christianity consider heterosexuality as the default. Men's work was more satisfying and important, so of course their brotherly love was greater than anything associated with women. To be honest, we need examples of mutual male affection because of all the homophobic rhetoric that exists around us. Men grow up in the West taught they can't even be affectionate with their fathers or brothers, much less their friends. For a brief period at the campus ministry I serve, we had a cadre of men across sexualities who were incredibly comfortable hugging, cuddling, and leaning on shoulders, and it was delightful to see. So I'm enchanted by the archiving of David and Jonathan's gentle physical touch and of their loving friendship in a scripture that, nine times out of ten, is about masculine violence. Their example is necessary to healthy relationships. And I adore the idea of David and Jonathan being best bros, hugging and weeping and fighting each other's enemies.

That said, the text is not as clear as many would like. The love they share, even in Hebrew, has implications of more than friendship. That scripture has been revised significantly over the centuries and their ambiguous relationship has been handed to us in this form speaks of something significant. In their time, homosexual connection certainly existed but was understood poorly and was condemned if for no other reason than it being a waste of the seed that contained children. Their relationship has been seen by queer people across centuries as representing their own love. So many lovers have lived together their whole lives with those outside speaking only of their close friendship or of their confirmed bachelorhood. Just search for photos and articles about Cary Grant and Randolph Scott and tell me they weren't a couple. Search for Gilgamesh and Enkidu and read about how they loved each other as husband and wife. Search for the Ladies of Llangollen and their life in Wales or the concept of Boston marriages. Just under the surface of what people want to see is what actually is. And gay men in particular seeing themselves in heroic characters—in passionate and intelligent and successful characters, in characters with value—is everything.

We don't know for certain what David and Jonathan's relationship was meant to be in the story. Obviously, I lean toward the two of them being romantically involved, but I'm comfortable sitting in ambiguity, so long as a romantic relationship is one of the possibilities. To Michal, it doesn't matter much whether they were friends or lovers because David turned away from her and toward her brother Jonathan. The *why* is immaterial, particularly in the buildup of pain and resentment. She might have hated her brother in the end as well, but we only have her conversation with David, and I wonder if some of her anger at him wasn't blame for her brother's death.

"Why," I hear you say, "are you spending so much time on a dude in a book about women in the Bible?" I'll level with you—this chapter began life as a study of Michal and Abigail and evolved into some rambling about all of David's women, but I found I had nothing to say about the two of them. I was constantly drawn to Jonathan and to the complex relationships these two siblings had with the same man. And as much as I want desperately to bring women's stories to people's consciousness, there's so much intersection between how women's stories and queer stories have been treated by the male power structure. Both have been erased, ignored, and abused by scripture and history; neither has been ascribed the significance they deserve by those with the authority to do so.

You might very well say that words like *gay* and *queer* didn't mean then what they mean now, that sexual identity shifts across culture and generations, and you'd be right. We certainly can't know what precisely was in David's and Jonathan's hearts, how they would have described themselves, and how that would have meshed with modern terminology. Yet queer people have existed—lesbian, gay, bisexual, trans, and nonbinary people—since there have been humans, just as surely as women and men have existed, and their reported behavior suggests that there is more than one interpretation. More than all this, my whole point in these books is that we need each other's stories, and we need the messiness of not knowing precisely what the story is, who is attracted to who, or precisely what genitals someone has. The details of those stories and their uncertainties are deeply important for us to name out loud, just as much as the universality of their struggles.

One of my students at the campus ministry I serve was trying to put into words how she felt about the person she was dating, and it was a bit of a word salad: *messy*. We talked about just saying the thing and asking for the other person's thoughts and feelings in return, not worrying about crafting the perfect, precise description. I said, "What about 'I have vague and messy positive feelings toward you'?"

I feel like Jonathan and Michal could say that to each other and, with varying inflections, to David. Uncertainty and imperfection are very much a part of their relationships and all of ours as well. David is not an unadulterated hero; Michal isn't entirely immature and demanding; Jonathan seems straightforward, but is he really risking his life solely for God's ordination of a Davidic political dynasty? In the end, Michal and Jonathan could be in the ambiguous space between being pawns in a larger game and making their own forceful choices. Again, it's messy. Perhaps it was a relief to Michal to live as a widow, out of the spotlight, where she could treasure all these things and ponder them in her heart.

9

The Queen of Sheba

More Than Meets the Eye

> King Solomon gave to the queen of Sheba every desire
> that she expressed, as well as what he gave her out of
> Solomon's royal bounty.
>
> —1 KINGS 10:13

There was a queen, dark and lovely, in the nation of Sheba. She was wealthier than the wealthiest men, more generous than the most generous men, and wiser than the wisest men. She was a woman of compassion and curiosity, a woman who approached the world with wide-open eyes. Her name was Bilqis if you heard her stories from your Muslim family, or else it was Makeda if you heard them from your Ethiopian and Coptic family. (I lean toward calling her Makeda, since scholars think Sheba was located in modern-day Ethiopia.) This queen in Sheba heard that the king in Israel was much renowned for his wealth, generosity, and wisdom, so she resolved to visit him. She packed up crates and crates of jewels, of paintings so beautiful they would make you weep, of finely woven cloths so soft the hair on your arms would raise at the barest touch, of spices—cinnamon, turmeric, cumin, and cloves, of course, but also spices you've never in your long life even heard of and whose names you cannot pronounce—and a chair, intricately carved from a single piece of wood and delicately inlaid with silver.

She left Sheba with hundreds of camels and thousands of servants and courtiers to meet with King Solomon.

Makeda, the Queen of Sheba, arrived in Jerusalem and was met with great rejoicing and much curiosity—who was this exotic woman who sparkled when she moved and smelled of cardamom from twenty feet off? When Makeda arrived in Jerusalem to give King Solomon gifts and ask him hard questions, he met her on the steps of the palace, a smile on his face. He'd heard of her wealth and generosity and wisdom, and he was eager to meet her as well. As they talked in the gardens and over dinner and in the halls, his eyes sparkled at her wit and perception. What a woman, he thought to himself, with such beautiful black skin and knowing eyes, such grace in her step and word. He answered every question she asked, often with questions of his own. Later, folk retold the story saying Solomon had answers for her every question, Solomon's wit astounded her, Solomon maintained his manly composure in her presence while only she was full of questions and awe, but we know the truth. We know this was a meeting of great minds, of curious people dancing around each other and delving into the richness of the other.

They talked long into the night and through the following day. They rested apart for a time and then continued, telling jokes, asking riddles, working out what could be done about the problems facing each of their kingdoms, exploring the differences between their faiths. He was fascinated by the great quantity and variety of spices she'd brought—how are these used, where did they come from, how were they discovered? She was intrigued by just how many servants he had and, even more, how many wives he had, how the palace was at once opulent and hospitable, how he paused every so often to make offerings to his God. It was, in a brief few days, a kind of obsession between them—who *are* you and *how* are you and everything you do so enchanting?

One evening, after they had spent hours telling stories, both false and true, they sat slumped comfortably at a table, a bottle of fine wine between them. She rested her cheek in her hand, her stack of gold bracelets clinking quietly, and let out a deep sigh of contentment. She said, "I find myself breathless listening to you, talking with you, making you laugh. I feel giddy with it." He said, "My dear, I feel quite the same." And she said, "I couldn't believe—I was ready to believe, you understand, I just could not conceive of a man so much my equal in ability and wisdom, and yet here you are! How happy your people must be to have you; how happy your many, many wives must be to live in your house. How happy your God must be to have blessed you so— your God who is clearly on the move across this land of yours like the scent of lilies on the breeze."

She was so intrigued by King Solomon that the weight and variety of spices she gave him on that visit have not been seen since—

It's right about here that, in the midst of their heady conversation, the writers and editors of this book and the almost entirely verbatim Chronicles following it saw fit to interrupt. They offer a quick reminder that it wasn't just Makeda who brought gifts to King Solomon but also Hiram, a man whom Solomon clearly had no sensual or personal interest in, that all of these gifts were purely platonic. Kind of a scriptural and literary cockblock. Ahem, carry on.

—and in response, King Solomon touched her cheek gently, so gently that the hairs on her arm stood up and it felt like lightning moving across her skin, and he offered her everything she desired, everything he could give her beyond his wisdom and generosity, everything in his heart and in his bed. He offered, and she received.

And that's it. There are a precious twelve or thirteen verses devoted to the Queen of Sheba, a goldmine of innuendo and suggestion. She shows up once more when loosely referenced in the Christian gospels as the Queen of the South. Jesus of Nazareth was offering wisdom sayings and getting irritated with the religious authority, and he brought her up along with Jonah (of whale and whining fame) as short stories showing great wisdom and transformation, though still less than his own. It's possible that she is the female narrator of the Song of Songs, that great erotic poem enshrined in scripture as an allegory for the love between God and the people but which is so much more than mere allegory. Over two thousand years' worth of legends have grown up around her, an entire country traces its lineage back to her, marital traditions and classic art revolving around this one seemingly straightforward story. She came, she saw, she discussed, she dropped off a pile of gold and spices, she left. So many commentaries talk about this story through the lens of Solomon: Solomon's wisdom, Solomon's wealth, Solomon's networking, and Makeda is only an example of those things, pleasing to look upon but not anyone to concern ourselves with. And thus I do concern myself with her.

First, those "hard questions" she put to Solomon: they're literally riddles, so it amuses me to think of them eating ridiculously fancy foods, being fanned by servants with palm leaves, and asking each other, "Say my name and I disappear. What am I?" Or "How is a raven like a writing desk?" But it's the same word in Hebrew as Samson's terrible lion carcass riddle and Daniel's interpreting Nebuchadnezzar's dreams—they're not just word puzzles. There's something weighty in each conversation, something of import. And, you'll notice, they talk about everything: "all that was on her mind," "all her questions," "there was nothing hidden from the king," and "all the wisdom of Solomon" (1 Kings 10:2–4). No wonder she was breathless at the end of it. The story is about her mind as much as it is about the riches she brings. Though the riches are indeed a powerful incentive for folk then and now to pay attention to her—that much hasn't changed. But because her mind is so perceptive, so willing to hear and examine, she acknowledges the God of Israel as the true God.

You may have noticed my unsubtle reference to Makeda and Solomon's lovemaking. It's because scripture isn't particularly subtle and because this is one of the things pretty much everyone writes about: Did they or didn't they? The Ethiopian Coptic Church says yes, they absolutely did—it was glorious, and their son Menelik was the progenitor of all Ethiopians. (Fascinatingly,

Rastafarians also claim Makeda and Solomon as ancestors.) Some rabbis say Solomon had "criminal intercourse" (rape) with her, and Nebuchadnezzar, the Babylonian king who took Israel into Exile, was the child of this rape. That story strikes me as a way to "make sense" of something that already makes perfect sense. It reminds me of my irritation with the ending of *Star Wars: The Rise of Skywalker*—not everyone has to be connected to some named or famous character. Some people are just people. And there are those who would say they absolutely did not have sex, rather like Sarah being untouched both times Abraham let her be taken into another man's house and bed. The Talmud goes so far as to say she didn't even exist, that it was a delegation of men from the kingdom of Sheba who visited. As an outsider to Judaism, I have to take this interpretation seriously, but I also have to ask if it's not an attempt to erase her and to specifically discredit the stories about their lovemaking.

The Ethiopian Church goes even further to say that their son Menelik returned to Israel to be anointed king of Ethiopia by the high priest Zadok, and upon leaving, his servants stole the Ark of the Covenant, the sacred case containing the Torah that the Israelites carried into Canaan, from the Temple. They say it sits to this day in a church in Ethiopia that only one priest is allowed to enter. They say that Solomon gave chase but failed to catch them and so gave orders that a copy of the Ark should be placed in the Temple so they wouldn't look like fools.

Muslims have their own stories about Makeda, or Bilqis as they call her. King Solomon is held in high regard in the Qur'an but as more of a wizard king, his court full of jinn and magic. He heard from a bird that an intriguing woman had taken the throne in the South, so he used his magical arts to get her to visit. Some stories say that didn't work but she was fascinated by him nonetheless and made the journey. There was a rumor he'd heard that she had the legs of a donkey, hairy and hooved, so when she arrived, he made the floor of the palace so smooth it looked like still water. She lifted her skirts to avoid getting them wet as she crossed, but in doing so, she revealed her ignorance and also her donkey legs, or perhaps just normal, hairy, human legs. One version of that story has Solomon inventing Nair so that the "shame" of her hair was removed. Then she asked him three to six riddles to test his wisdom ("What's black and white and red all over?") that he answered perfectly. The revealing of her body became the revealing of her mind and heart as she converted to the worship of Allah. Yet another story says she was the daughter of a snake princess and had snakey legs that, again, Solomon cured, leading to her conversion. Again, as an outsider to Islam, I can't reject these stories out of hand, but I can't help but ask, What if her legs were perfectly normal and she and others seemed to think they were hideously deformed, like some versions of the Fantastic Four's nemesis Victor Von Doom? What if women's bodies don't need to be altered to be found beautiful and she was stunning as she was? What if Solomon did heal her, but it was the kind of healing we all experience when we are truly seen and loved as we are?

The Medieval Church had a thousand ways to shoehorn the Christian story into Jewish texts, and this one is no exception. One story says that as Makeda approached Jerusalem, she had to cross a bridge just below the Temple but refused to do so and knelt in prayer beside it instead. We are told it's because she intuited that this very bridge would one day become the cross on which Jesus of Nazareth would be crucified. (See my earlier irritation vis-à-vis Star Wars.) Another story says the spices she brought were gold, frankincense, and myrrh. And it's this era in which the church became enamored of Solomon as a prototype for Christ and Makeda for the church, loving and making love in bridal mysticism. Their meeting is depicted in so many paintings like a wedding procession, her gifts to him her dowry and their union opening up the gates of heaven. In those same paintings, she can often be seen with a webbed foot, a picture telephone version of the donkey legs she might have had.

The thing is, she is exotic and sexy. She is Black and beautiful (note, not Black *but* beautiful as the Song of Songs says, as though Blackness is something incompatible with beauty). Look up model Nyakim Gatwech sometime and be awed by her beauty. The great wealth the Queen of Sheba brought, the great mind in her head, and the obvious enjoyment she and Solomon found in each other are unproblematic, a rarity for a biblical woman. That is, nothing bad happened because of or to her in the story. Fertility was not at stake, she was not stigmatized, the relationship between God and God's people was not threatened, it was all just lovely, including the implied lovemaking. But outside of the story, she is a woman whose body, whose physical presence, was sensual and dangerous. The story itself deals only with her exoticism. It is later that people read the story that her "feet" (a common euphemism inside and outside of scripture for genitals so that polite people could talk about impolite things) were made horrifying by attaching them to hairy legs, her comeliness negated by her Blackness. Improper sexual relations, both the marrying of non-Israelite women and other miscellaneous, not-strictly-missionary-position variations, are metaphors for the worship of foreign gods in much of the Hebrew scriptures. Women, every one of them, make us drunk with arousal simply by existing, so we must control it; we must control them.

Makeda is an outsider, which scripture is ambivalent about. Sometimes it's a major liability for Israel, as when prophets warn the people (the male people, of course) to send away their foreign wives and children who have been corrupting them. Sometimes it's neutral, as Solomon's thousands of foreign wives and his platform of progressive pluralism seem to be. He didn't only build them houses; he built them temples to their own gods, which the Bible reports without emotion. It's not until his twilight years that it was a problem, when he turned to those other gods and away from Yahweh. Sometimes being an outsider is even wildly positive, as in the story of Ruth and Naomi or Tamar or this Queen of Sheba. Being a stranger, in so much of scripture, means an opportunity to be welcomed as much as one to be feared. Makeda was from the Far South, like the *magi* were from the Far East: people from distant lands, heathen lands, lands that couldn't possibly have known about Yahweh, came flocking to Israel to acknowledge Solomon's and Israel's and Yahweh's greatness. She was outside the faith, outside "normal" women's activity. She was fascinating and repulsive and you couldn't look away.

Stories about outsiders who couldn't possibly understand, who had never heard of God or Jesus, yet repenting and worshipping, are the stock and trade of so many churches. They assume all people on the outside of our faith looking in want and need this conversion, that by not being Jewish or eventually Christian or Muslim, folks are doomed to their strangeness and outsiderness with no other positive options. Christians, specifically, so often look at atheists and agnostics with pity and mystification: How could they be loving or moral people without our particular God? Friends, some of the most kind, most just, most godly people I know are atheists.

I'm sure you have a whole cast of characters in your own life whom you might describe as outsiders. Perhaps they're the poor or disenfranchised, perhaps they're from other countries seeking a better life, perhaps they're criminals or conspiracy theorists. Perhaps you and your friends understand yourselves as outsiders to an uncaring system. *Outsiderness*, if I may coin a word, can be interpreted as a threat or a gift. Simply being outside of the norm is neither necessarily healthy nor unhealthy—cancer is outside of the norm, genius is outside of the norm—discernment is necessary. But that's just it: turning away wholesale from those we think of as outsiders is no discernment and is inhumane. Did you know that the edges of a farm where the field meets the trees are the spaces most full of life? Of course there can be predators there, of course it can be dangerous, but it also enriches the entire farm. The Queen of Sheba is like this—a glorious, exciting example of welcoming in the outsider who enriches all our lives when we do so.

They're such brief passages in the canon of scripture, her stories, and such involved storytelling afterward. You don't continue to create stories about someone because they mean nothing to you. Makeda, the Queen of Sheba, still speaks to us. She is, to me, a woman I didn't know I was emulating. Not with the crates of jewels and spices, but in searching out a person who would be my peer and partner. I didn't really know there was another option, to be honest. I only knew that I wanted a spouse and lover who would love my mind and heart as much as my body, someone who would make me laugh long and loud, someone who would see how much of an outsider I feel myself to be and invite me in. She has been cheering me on my whole life and I had no idea.

The Queen of Sheba, with her fragrant and flagrant sexuality, with her willingness to explore and listen and challenge and relish, might just be the hero we need right now. She is our fairy godmother sprinkling us with sparkles and possibility, our mentor, our confidante. She is the drag queens of the Sisters of Perpetual Indulgence; she is Josephine Baker and Audrey Hepburn, heroes of World War II; she is Dolly Parton singing and laughing and giving away her fortune. We can't forget her because she's still here.

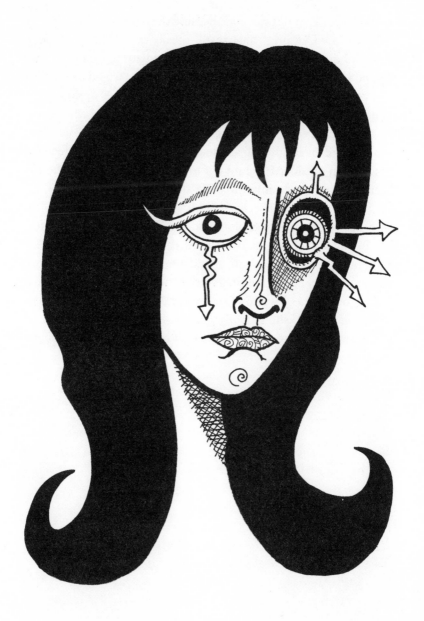

Jezebel

No More Evil Than the Next Guy

His wife Jezebel said to him, "Do you now govern Israel?
Get up, eat some food, and be cheerful; I will give you the
vineyard of Naboth the Jezreelite."

— 1 KINGS 21:7

Ok, listen: it's Jezebel. We all know she's evil. Violent and sexually aggressive and witchy and a bad influence on the young people of today. Like that one girl our moms warned us about. Or that one woman we never got over, damn her. I get it. Except she's not. I'm not saying she's a paragon of virtue we should all emulate like Susanna or Mary Magdalene (go read *Fierce* and come back if you think I'm being sarcastic here). I'm saying she's not the slag we think. She's got her own complex motivations and feelings, and the narrator telling us her story in 1 and 2 Kings has his own complex motivations and feelings. And insecurities and projections. Just saying.

Jezebel, daughter of Sidonian King Ethbaal, was a devoted wife to a husband she didn't intend to marry but grew to care for. She was a woman of determination and strength who got shit done. She was a proud woman, knowing her value and station, walking with her chin up and shoulders back. She was unbowed, untamed, and fierce. She had a driving passion for her faith, did everything in her power to protect her people, and was a hero, really. She *did* have her enemies murdered, but what king didn't? And she did worship Baal and Asherah rather than Yahweh, but we don't need to hold that against her, right?

Scripture sure does. It's her prime iniquity that she didn't convert to Judaism and acknowledge Yahweh as the only God when she married King Ahab, despite "foreign wives" never being required to do so in other books. King Solomon's many, many wives didn't convert, and he even built them temples to their gods, which, in the telling of it, scripture does not condemn. Solomon himself, just a few chapters before we meet Jezebel, was castigated for his own giving in and worshipping his wives' gods, but the wives themselves are not mentioned. Think of it like a noncompete clause: Solomon signed one, the wives didn't. Jezebel's name even gives away the plot: her feud with the prophet Elijah was over which God was real and the true winner. His name means "my God is Yahweh," hers "Baal exalts." It's a cosmic and mythic battle between Yahweh and Baal, between Judah and everyone else.

But first, it's just a story about a woman in an arranged marriage to cement a political alliance. Princess Jezebel of Sidon showed up in Israel with a suitcase and a dream, the result of King Ahab's love affair with Baal, not the cause of it. She did not use her feminine wiles to turn his head—his head was already turned. Which I suppose was a pleasant surprise to her, easing the transition. Her dad King Ethbaal had seen Ahab's fascination and purchased his loyalty with Jezebel as the currency.

Her new husband Ahab had built altars to Baal and put up sacred poles to Asherah and then married her, a captivating woman from his new faith. A little on the nose there, Ahab. In the secular world, history books tell us, he was successful in foreign policy, helping neighboring nations defeat the invading Assyrians. The writer of the books of Kings is deeply embarrassed by all of this and insists that Ahab was more evil than any of his predecessors. They say Ahab sacrificed his son Segub so that his rebuilding of Jericho would be successful, so it's not entirely unfair. But need I remind you that the predecessors of the kings of Israel were the judges, and there was that one particular judge who offered his wife-slash-concubine to be gang-raped for hours and then chopped her up and sent the bits out to the tribes to show how much he himself had been wronged by the rapists? But for the purposes of the larger story, sure, Ahab was very, very bad.

Anyway, they got married in a lovely Baal-and-Asherah-themed ceremony with baby pink and teal table decorations, and they went off to rule Israel. Almost immediately—narratively, anyway—there was a drought in the land. Drought, you understand, wasn't just the parched dryness of no rain; it was God's displeasure with the people, a kind of divine "go to your room and think about what you've done." It was also the physical embodiment of God's impotence: "Is God real if this is happening to us?" Don't judge. When assholes shoot up elementary schools or our beloved mothers are diagnosed with cancer, we ask the exact same questions—we're not so different. The drought lasted three years, and I imagine it was all Jezebel and Ahab could do to keep the nation functioning, to keep some of the people alive, regardless of who they worshipped. Later it says Jezebel fed four hundred prophets of Asherah at her table—she supported them financially, which makes sense, but given the context, she may also have literally been feeding them, soup-kitchen style. What a honeymoon.

In her spare time, Jezebel had been busy killing off the prophets of Yahweh. Or having them killed, really; she had people for that kind of business. It's a matter-of-fact statement—we all know she's had people killed; it's all over the talk shows—from a character called Obadiah. He's only in the story so we the readers can see how ridiculous and smarmy the narrator thinks it is to find a middle way between complete obedience to Yahweh and disinterest. *Pick a side*, the narrator says. Why would Jezebel do this? She was a polytheist, so there must have been room in her pantheon for Yahweh, particularly as so much of his character was similar to Baal and the elder god El. She wouldn't have had any need to destroy followers of another god—the more the merrier! Unless

someone had been busy killing off the Baal and Asherah prophets first. Brings to mind the iconic scene in Star Wars when Han
Solo pulls his gun and shoots Greedo—who shot first? Spoilers,
it's Han. Here it might very well be Elijah. Violence begetting
violence comes as no surprise, and it seems unlikely Jezebel was
the aggressor here.

Even so, she was acting like Joshua did with the Canaanites,
like Haman wanted Ahasuerus to do and Esther's people actually
did, like the czars did in the pogroms, like white folk did with
nooses during America's Jim Crow era: eliminate the opposition.
And Elijah, Man of God as it said on his business cards, did the
same in response, but his action was described as virtuous and
hers heinous. At Mt. Carmel, Elijah won a competitive animal-
sacrifice event he'd set up that was more Vegas-style magic show
than trustworthy theology. He pitted himself against 450 prophets
of Baal and 400 prophets of Asherah, and "all Israel" was there to
watch the bout. Were there popcorn and beer vendors winding
through the crowd? Pita and wine? The prophets of Baal marched
and chanted and wailed all day—it was very entertaining—and
nothing happened. Meanwhile, Elijah trash-talked them, saying
their god must be napping or on the potty. When it was his turn,
he poured so much water on the altar that nothing could possibly
catch fire and there was a small river around it. But at a dramatic
word and gesture from Elijah, a bolt of fire from the heavens con-
sumed everything in the area: meat, wood, stone, dust, and water.
Astounding! And proof! Proof of Yahweh's supremacy. And then
Elijah killed all 450 prophets of Baal as was apparently right and
proper. If we're judging Jezebel solely on her violence, Elijah,
beloved and chosen by God, has her beat by a mile. He may also
have been more of a drama queen.

It's only after he spilled the blood of the prophets that it
rained.

Queen Jezebel was not well-pleased by this. The rain, she was
grateful for, but this feud, the death? No, not pleased at all. She
wrote him a letter saying, "Boy, you better run!" and he did.

She had real power in this kingdom, and he took it seriously. He hid himself away in the wilderness and later a cave. He told Yahweh that Israel had forsaken him—not Jezebel, you'll notice, it's not her fault, but Israel as a whole—and then poetically, and a little self-pityingly, he said, "I alone am left and they are seeking my life." It's a rough gig being the prophet of Yahweh. He and Jeremiah might have gotten along well.

In the middle of this epic struggle between Elijah and Jezebel and Yahweh and Baal, there's a story of Jezebel and Ahab's domestic life and practices that would be quaint if not for the deception and contract killing. (Interestingly, earlier versions of this book don't include Jezebel in this story at all—later editors added her in as proof of their theory that marrying foreign wives led to evil. Fabricate evidence of what you already think? Sure.) A man named Naboth owned a vineyard next-door to the palace, and Ahab wanted it so he could plant a little garden. Some peppers and tomatoes, maybe try his hand at garlic. But Naboth, that jerk, said, "No, it's been in my family for generations, and you know how important that is in our culture and point in history, man." So King Ahab went home and threw himself facedown on the bed feeling sorry for himself and sighing piteously. Seriously, scripture says he was resentful and sullen and wouldn't eat because of it. His wife Jezebel saw him lying there with his socked feet sticking off the end of the bed and asked, "Why are you sulking, man?" And when he told her that Naboth was mean to him and wouldn't give him the vineyard even though he said he'd give him some other very cool stuff, she said, "Dude, you're king—you can do what you want. Do I have to do everything? Go have a snack or something." Or maybe it was more like, "Oh, babe, what's wrong? Why are you so sad? Oh, I'll get you what you need, honey bear." Perhaps she stroked his hair or his back while he poured his heart out about how he just needed a place where he could be Ahab, not the king. It's hard to tell from the text if she's mocking or solicitous.

Either way, she wrote letters in the king's name—unquestioned but also unlikely they didn't know it was her—to arrange for a legal murder, rather like King David sending his lover's husband to the front line of the war so he'd die and David could keep his paramour. Jezebel got two unsavory people to accuse Naboth of cursing both Yahweh and Ahab, and because there were two witnesses, the law couldn't question it—one person could lie, sure, but two? Impossible. So poor old Naboth was stoned to death. Ahab got what he wanted, their marriage was strengthened, everybody wins.

Of course, you might also be reminded of the story of Susanna in the Apocrypha who was falsely accused in court by two lecherous, old men who wanted to see her naked. Not just any lecherous, old men but elders—people who had been given care of the community, who were meant to protect and serve the people. These were men with authority who abused that authority to get what they wanted. Remind you of some drug companies, Congress, hedge funds? *This* is idolatry, this is greed and self-interest, this worship of power. This, it seems to me, was Jezebel's real sin. Not to minimize the hundreds she had killed, but it's the *why*: it's the offhandedness with which she did any of it. And Elijah as well. And all the kings. It's the lightness with which they held other people's lives, the entitlement to riches and being right.

Elijah soon prophesied that Ahab's blood would be licked from the ground by dogs and, worse, that Jezebel would be entirely eaten by dogs, but it was slow to come to fruition. It was three years later that Ahab entered an ill-advised war and died, leaving their son Ahaziah to be king after him. (For those playing along at home, we are told dogs did indeed lick his blood up from the floor of his chariot.) After another two years, Ahaziah—also a big fan of Baal and Asherah—died and was followed by his brother Jehoram, who ruled for twelve years. (This is all made a bit confusing because various synchronous kings in Israel and Judah have the same names.) All the while, Jezebel was still alive. Eventually, a new king named Jehu was anointed and set his sights on Jezebel. She was a symbol of Israel's corporate sin, and ironically, she was even more powerful now that she was the Queen Mum.

On his way, Jehu complained of Jezebel's witchcraft and whore-doms, the first and last time either of these things is mentioned. Sexual metaphors are frequently used for Israel's relationship with Yahweh—being a faithful wife, God taking Israel into their bed, Israel having many affairs with other nations who are better-hung than horses—so it was widely understood that Jehu was referring to her worship of Baal rather than literal whoring. In fairness to her, she had never been unfaithful to Yahweh because they were never in a relationship in the first place. It's like being deeply wounded that a person in your neighborhood is cheating on someone else's husband. Israel was constantly flirting with other gods; Jezebel is laudable for her loyalty to her own. Again, in focusing on Jezebel the way it does, the text shows its antiforeigner, antiwoman, and particularly antiwoman-in-power agenda.

But generations of interpreters have taken the whore imag-ery and run with it, particularly because when she heard Jehu was on his way to kill her, Jezebel put on makeup and dressed up. She must have been sexually aggressive and promiscuous to do that—there could be no other explanation. I know I have never put on my fancy clothes and done my hair for any other reason than to whore it up, have you? No, sometimes we just like to dress up. Sometimes it's battle armor. One time, because I knew a pain-ful phone conversation was coming, I put on my sharpest winged eyeliner as a form of defense. (It worked: I rocked it.) Why was Jezebel's costume seen differently than, say, Esther's? Or Tamar's? Elijah, Man of God, wore ugly haircloth and a leather belt—why couldn't she be dowdier like him and show her humiliation? She was not particularly sexual, unless the mere presence of a woman means arousal and sexual activity. Which it doesn't, but some seem to think it does. Friends, she went to her end with her chin up and shoulders back, the way she lived her life. It's not vanity—it's comfort; it's protection.

But it didn't protect her. The eunuchs in her employ defenes-trated her (not a word you get to use very often), and Elijah's pre-diction came true: the dogs ate her body so that all that was left when they went to bury her was her skull, her feet, and the palms of her hands—fascinating and disgusting. After he killed Jezebel, Jehu had all seventy of Ahab's other sons killed, then "all who were left of Ahab's house," then another forty-two of Ahaziah's relatives, then all the rest of Ahab's people in Samaria, and finally, by pretending to have a feast for Baal, every last one of the Baal-worshippers in Israel because of his zeal for Yahweh. Yay?

Does it feel like I'm being too hard on these folks? It was a rough time to be alive by all accounts, including nonbiblical ones. It was a more violent and precarious time, even than now in the midst of the coronavirus pandemic and state-sponsored brutality, so perhaps we can't judge these folks as harshly as we'd like for the death they're dealing and reporting. But if that's the case, we can't blame Jezebel any more than we can the other rulers—comparatively, she deals rather minimal death. Still, the text uses her as an example of what happens to a nation when they abandon Yahweh. She is, both for Ahab and for the whole nation, the result of their own unfaithfulness, not the cause. A foreign woman on the throne, essentially ruling in the place of her weaker husband—how could the country be brought this low? This is yet another example among many of how Israel and its twin sister Judah to the south must have brought on their own annihilation at the hands of Babylon.

Wait, what?

It's that whole other overarching story I've mentioned before going on simultaneously with the writing of this one and all the others in the Hebrew scriptures: the story of the Exile. It's like all the stories you know—creation, Exodus, Joseph, Tamar, the exhaustive rules in Leviticus—they're all the individual food items on your dinner plate, and the Exile is the chef who combined them in just this way. The short version is this: in 586 BCE, Babylon invaded Judah, destroyed the Temple in Jerusalem, and carried off all the rulers, scholars, businesspeople, and influencers into captivity. I don't know if you caught that—they *destroyed the Temple*. Where God lived. That Temple was razed. So where was God?

Had . . . had God died? Or had God let this happen? How could the people created and loved and chosen by God be done this way? What did they do to deserve it? For fifty years, they wondered and pondered and made a new life in Babylon. "This is the new normal, I guess," they said. And then Babylon in turn was invaded by Persia, and King Cyrus sent them all home to Judah. A new, new normal, which was also extremely difficult and confusing. What to make of all of this? Who is God and what in the world is God doing? That's the question that scripture tries to answer. The facts were written down in retrospect and are at the service of theology.

I share this because Jezebel was written this way as part of this meaning-making, this attempt to understand how this destruction could have happened. This writer, often called the Deuteronomistic Historian, believes in "military punishment for religious faithlessness," according to one scholar. In other words, Israel and Judah *deserved* this disaster because they turned their backs on Yahweh. Jezebel and almost every other king are only signs, symbols of the faithlessness that pervaded every person there. More than that, what this historian is doing through the lens of redemptive violence is trying to help the people work through generational trauma. Think about the trauma Black people in America experience in their thoughts, their hearts, and their bodies—it's a result of decades and centuries of abuse from white supremacist culture. Think about the trauma people whose families have lived in poverty for decades experience. Of course there are stories of folks healing and coming out of these situations, but they carry with them the weight and pain of the past. That weight doesn't just disappear because they get a good job. It doesn't just disappear because slavery "ends." It doesn't just end because they're back from Exile. This is all trauma, and it sticks around.

From that perspective—trying to find the through line to explain how we got here, wherever *here* is—fair enough. Except not fair to Jezebel as a person, not fair to the countless women who have been condemned as Jezebels or executed as witches for knowing what they want, for being sensual or proud of their bodies and their work. God, scripture tells us, is a jealous God, desiring with their whole being our love and attention, jealous to the point of violence against their own people when they stray. And this violence attributed to God as righteous punishment, it's perpetrated not by God but by people. We are the ones hurting each other ostensibly to make things better. But violence isn't redemptive. It might be cathartic, it might feel good at times, it might feel like the only possible answer in the face of overwhelming odds, but it is never redemptive.

Regardless of her morality, Jezebel is a woman caught between men, like so many others. Like the concubine in Judges. Like Tamar. She is wife of Ahab, daughter of Ethbaal, nemesis of Elijah, queen and princess. She is the prey of Jehu and the scapegoat of historians and theologians for centuries. And she is not silent.

Recently, I've been going to a lot of protests for racial equality and an end to police brutality. I am so encouraged by how many people—and how many white people—are in the streets this time. And I am also so disappointed by the leadership of my city and my country. We march and we write letters and we show up for budget hearings and it's like we didn't even bother. Except for the protesters in jail and the fading words painted on blacktop, "Black lives matter." Like the prophets of Baal and Asherah, it often feels like we are marching and chanting and wailing all day for weeks and months and centuries and nothing happens. Like Jezebel, it feels like we are standing up for what gives life, for the truth as we see it, and we are not just being ignored; we are being criminalized.

Jezebel was no saint, and like Asherah, I'm not asking that we lionize her. But I am asking us to see how we demonize people we don't understand. I am asking that we pay attention to our own unfaithfulness to the things we hold dear. Jezebel's story doesn't call us to be nice—nice means nothing. We are called to be faithful, and we are called to be faithful like she was. Like Elijah was. In the end, like Eve eating the fruit of the knowledge of good and evil, they all know they will die, and they grieve that ending and try to make meaning out of what they have.

11

Huldah and the Three Wise Women

> The woman said to Joab, "His head shall be thrown over the wall to you." Then the woman went to all the people with her wise plan. And they cut off the head of Sheba son of Bichri, and threw it out to Joab.
>
> —2 SAMUEL 20:21–22

Listen, did you know that the title "Three Wise Men" is not even slightly mentioned in the Bible? The word Matthew uses there is *magi*, and it means "magicians"—that is, more than one mage. No genders are specified, no royalty, no numerical specificity. They were literally sorcerers from far away, and like the Medium of Endor and like Jacob and Laban and Rachel, their magic worked. They were able to discern through their arts that the heavens were telling them something and where that something was. In my family, we have as many magi in our nativity as the kids see fit to bring down from their stash of toys—this year it was at least twelve, and one was a stuffed baby seal. I digress, but only a little. The *magi* were wise, learned, and there to name the significance of other people's actions. So it is with these Three Wise Women and Huldah the prophet.

"I've never heard of women prophets," one of my students said recently. I mean, that's not surprising. Isaiah and Ezekiel and

Jeremiah have kind of a monopoly on our brain space, so we don't remember that the old lady Anna who cooed over the baby Jesus or that Miriam, the sister of Moses, were prophets. To be fair, there aren't many of them, and some were more adjacent to the power structure than part of it—functional prophets but not wearing the official, sequined mantle. Huldah was one with the title; the Wise Women of Endor, Tekoa, and Abel were some of those without. Their wisdom and their magic, even, brought clarity and transformation.

First, there's the Medium of Endor. She sounds like a pulpy fantasy novel or a Star Wars spin-off, but she was an actual sorcerer. Some translations of the Bible call her a witch, but that's inaccurate as well as mysogynist. Witches in the Western world were women who had their own visions of how to live an abundant life or who were convenient scapegoats for other people's pain. No, the Medium of Endor was a spiritualist and a necromancer— literally someone who speaks with the dead—and her magic actually worked. Her job had been condemned and outlawed by the same king who then came to employ her services.

It was the late eleventh century BCE near the end of King Saul's reign, and he had been losing consistently—militarily, politically, socially, even. He was, perhaps for the first time, afraid. There was a battle on the horizon with the Philistines, and he'd gone to ask God what would happen. Silence. He could see the Philistines' encampment, their banners, their sentries lined up on the edge of the hill, and his fear increased. Who could he consult to tell him what to do? It came to him: his old advisor, the prophet Samuel. That guy would know exactly what to do. One problem: he was dead. But Saul was desperate and not a little bit hypocritical. He'd expelled all the mediums from Israel, back when he was still following the Law, but apparently, there was still one nearby, keeping her head down, doing her work quietly and only for those she trusted not to turn her in. So King Saul put on a disguise and went to her in the dead of night, so afraid was he.

The Medium of Endor, upon seeing someone she didn't know on her doorstep asking her to call up the spirit of someone long dead, said to him, "Dude, if I do this, the king'll kill me. Entrapment is what this is. No, thank you," and tried to close the door. He stuck his foot in and pleaded, "Lady, I swear to you on whatever you like I won't tell anyone. Please, please help me." She narrowed her eyes at him, considering whether to trust him, and asked, "Who do you want to talk to?" He said, "Samuel." And suddenly she realized who she was talking to. She recoiled, yelling, "What the hell, your majesty? You lied to me." He followed her in, trying to placate her with calming gestures, saying, "I won't punish you, I promise. Please, what do you see?" And, perhaps unable to stop the vision, she told him, "I see a god rising up from the ground like mist, an old man in a robe." Saul, knowing this was Samuel, prostrated himself on the ground, partly out of respect, partly out of relief. Here, now, Samuel would help him and things would change, he could feel it.

Samuel, dressed in what can only be described as raiment, radiating authority, said to Saul, "Why did you wake me up, young man?" Saul, groaning into the floor, said, "The Philistines are out there and God's not taking my calls and I don't know what to do." Samuel said, "Listen, I told you when I was alive that God would abandon you for David. I told you you're gonna lose. You've made your bed." What a thing to hear.

Saul lay on the floor, shuddering in fear and hunger and ennui. The medium tutted at him, rubbed his back, and said, "Oh, honey, I know. Let me make you a little something to eat." She was frustrated with Saul for his poor life decisions, but her heart still broke for him and his people. There's a part of me that imagines God doing the exact same thing. Saul is a right mess, and yet we have sympathy for him. The medium went out and killed a calf and made bread (no small task), and they ate together, meditatively, in silence, like the shawarma scene at the end of *The Avengers*. Earlier commentators have called her vile and dark and evil, maybe even leading Saul astray herself, but like so many other stories, that's not what it says at all. The Medium of Endor was just a person with a job, an unusual job to be sure, and one that used her gifts of wisdom and perception. The Medium of Endor acted as a midwife for an ending as much as a beginning.

Fairly soon after, in the early tenth century BCE and during King David's reign, there was the Wise Woman of Tekoa. She was acquainted with the king's right-hand man Joab, who saw that David was distracted from the kingdom by family matters. You see, David's firstborn son Amnon had manipulated, raped, and then abandoned his own half sister Tamar, sister of David's favorite son Absalom. But David had done nothing about it because he loved Amnon. Did he not love Tamar? Are men's desires so overpowering and their feelings and futures so important as to overshadow whatever they do? I don't believe that, but our cultures then and now tell us so. Absalom, though, was not so easily calmed. Two years later, he hired contract killers to do away with Amnon. David exiled Absalom, and we pick up the story three years later.

Joab, David's ever-practical yet ever-bloodthirsty general, saw that David's mind was stuck in a rut on Absalom, longing for him to return and still deeply angry. Joab may have cared for David, but mostly he was done with David mooning over his son. Joab, it says, called to a Wise Woman from the town of Tekoa and asked her to put on a performance akin to the one the prophet Nathan did when David had cheated himself into marrying Bathsheba. She put on a widow's costume and went to the king, asking for justice for her son: "He killed his brother, my other son, and though I am grieving, I am also afraid for him. My family says he must be killed as well for what he did, but how is that justice? Then I am grieving for two." King David listened to this with his compassionate face on and said, "Yes, of course I'll help you and try to protect him." Three times she pushed to get a clear commitment to save her remaining (fictional) son, refusing to let the law be the arbiter of justice. Finally, he said to her, "Look, lady, you have my word that your son will live and not die," to which she immediately replied, "Aha! You have said it yourself: How could you condemn your son to exile, a living death? You are like my (fictional) family—should you not do better?"

David, sometimes a bit slow on the uptake, said, "Did Joab put you up to this?" "He did," she said, and then, in words that feel more heartbreaking and more like her own, she said, "We must all die: we are like water spilled on the ground that cannot be gathered up." Perhaps she rested her hand on his shoulder or looked searchingly into his eyes for the awareness she hoped he had. She said, "Joab told me everything—about Amnon and Tamar and Absalom and about Jonathan and Michal. You don't have to keep up this cycle of punishment and violence. You can change things." And she said, "Every word I've said so far came from Joab." She said it, but I don't believe it. Maybe she was protecting herself from the king's probable anger at her ruse; maybe the writers of this story couldn't imagine a woman doing this on her own. Joab called on her because of her wisdom, her cunning. She wasn't just some old lady who said pithy things from time to time but a Wise Woman. Some dispute that this was an official title, but I'm inclined to disagree—he could have gotten any woman to play dress-up and deceive the king if he were going to tell her every single word to say, so why her? Because her wisdom was extraordinary, her ability to see clearly and to draw out the truth was startling, and people respected her. This Wise Woman was Joab's coconspirator in getting the king back to work.

Around the same time, there was the Wise Woman of Abel. She was a negotiator and a woman with authority. There was a troublemaker, scripture says, a scoundrel, or maybe he was more of an activist pushing back against a political regime that wasn't as great as everyone said it was. This man called Sheba went around telling people to leave off their support of King David, and "all of Israel" listened and walked away from David. In actuality, it was more likely just his family and friends, but he was making a ruckus, so King David sent his new right-hand man Amasa to take him out. Amasa didn't do it—because it takes time, because he didn't want to, because he was incompetent, we don't know—so David then sent a chunk of the army to do it. As a colorful aside, on their way to find Sheba, they came upon Amasa, and Joab approached him with a kiss of peace but shivved him instead and left him dying in the road with his intestines hanging out. This slowed their progress substantially, as all the troops and people rubbernecked on their way by.

Sheba had hidden himself in the town of Abel, so Joab prepared to destroy the whole city to get this guy. As the army was clanking around, building a siege ramp, putting their battering ram together, doing generally threatening army stuff, there came a woman's voice floating down from the wall: "Is General Joab out there? Let me speak to him." The soldiers all stopped what they were doing and listened. In the quiet, Joab came forward deferentially, for this was the voice of the Wise Woman of Abel. She said, "Are you Joab?" and he said, "Yes, ma'am." She said, "Are you listening?" He said, "Yes, ma'am, I am." She said, "Because this is important." He said, "I hear you."

The Wise Woman of Abel said, "People used to come here to Abel for wisdom, for prophecy, for advice during conflict. I am a peaceful woman, a faithful woman, and this city is peaceful and faithful, yet you're trying to destroy us. This city is a mother in Israel, and you will destroy our history if you destroy this city for want of one man. Is that what you want?" Joab looked ashamed but straightened his back: "Hell no, ma'am [profanity very much intended by the Hebrew], but there's this Sheba character who's hiding in there, and he's rebelling against the king, and we can't let that stand, ma'am." The Wise Woman said to the general, "I see. Hang on a moment and we'll toss his head over the wall to you." Ancient rabbis expanded on this part of the story, likening her to Abraham bargaining God down to finding only one righteous man in Sodom. They say she asked him if he'd accept one thousand dead men instead of the whole town and then bargained him down to just Sheba's life. Either way, she went to the people of the city with her "wise plan," and they agreed, beheaded him, and tossed his head over the wall, and everyone went about their merry way. Huzzah.

And much later, in the mid-seventh century BCE, there was Huldah. She's phenomenal, y'all. Huldah was a prophet—an officially recognized speaker for God, a truth teller, a political commentator, a dispenser of wisdom, a person with authority—often with a flair for the dramatic. She was also the first person to authenticate what would become Torah.

See, the people of Israel had been in and out of the Promised Land for generations, in and out of relationship with God, in and out of good behavior. They'd had trickster leaders, increasingly violent judges, and a series of kings who were, at best, a mixed blessing and, at worst, unadulterated buffoons. There came a time when those old kings died and a young man named Josiah came to the throne. I say young: he was eight. But he grew up well under the tutelage of his mother and the prophet Huldah. They taught him compassion and loyalty to the God of their ancestors, though apparently, they had no written record of this God or their ancestors. Josiah alone had the fortitude and willingness to truly transform Israel. As a young man of eighteen or so, he was already sending out troops of construction workers to tear down the poles and sacred groves dedicated to Asherah and the altars dedicated to her husband Baal. Their worship was ingrained in the people; their likenesses and their blessings were difficult to change. Imagine your own love of Jesus or a parent or your loyalty to a movement or comic book franchise and imagine someone in power telling you that it's not only morally wrong, it never existed in the first place. No, Josiah's faith and the faith of those who wrote down our scriptures were that Yahweh was the only god, not the best of a mixed bag, not an equal member of a pantheon, but the only one. Yet generations of Israelites had continued to worship Asherah and Baal alongside Yahweh, so he had his work cut out for him.

As part of this nationwide house cleaning, Josiah decided to renovate the Temple. The plaster was peeling, and the shag carpeting had seen better days. So Josiah deployed his troops of construction workers to spruce up the place, and while they were demoing walls to create the open concept they needed, they found an old scroll. They showed it to the high priest Hilkiah, who showed it to the king's advisors, who showed it to the king himself. They read it aloud (not a short task, since it was ostensibly all of the Torah—Genesis, Exodus, Leviticus, Numbers, and Deuteronomy), and King Josiah freaked right out because the people had not been following what this scroll said. Could it be real? How could they know? We are given to understand here that they didn't know they were supposed to act differently, that the generations of doing what was right in their own eyes were because the people of Israel had written down all of the Torah but then lost it. How could they have known how they were supposed to act? How could they have known what God was about? This scroll was, apparently, brand new information. So they took it to the only person wise enough to understand it: Huldah the prophet, wife of Shallum, the keeper of the king's wardrobe. (Unrelated to Huldah, I love that this job exists—it reminds me of all those movies about French royalty who have courtiers vying to be the one to hand over the royal skivvies.)

Huldah took one look and said, "This scroll is the real deal, and y'all should be afraid." She said, "God made a covenant with the people, and y'all have not been following it. Maybe a bit here and there, for kicks, but no, ever since the golden calf, ever since Sodom and Gomorrah, ever since the garden, y'all have been doing your own thing—hurting each other, hurting yourselves, ignoring the One Who Made Everything. Y'all deserve what's coming to you and so much more. Except for Josiah—he's alright." Ancient Jewish commentary says Josiah sent the scroll to Huldah because women were more merciful than men, which clearly backfired. And King Josiah, hearing her words, called all the people together in front of the Temple, half renovated as it was, and again read aloud all the words on the scroll—Genesis, Exodus, Leviticus,

Numbers, and Deuteronomy—and everyone wept and tore their clothes because they hadn't known.

Thereafter, Josiah got rid of all the other filthy religions, the people repented, and they all lived happily ever after. Except that Huldah was right, and it was too little, too late. They would all be taken into exile, their homes upended, their beautiful Temple destroyed, and their good King Josiah long dead.

Huldah is remembered for only a short moment, but a pivotal one. It was she who affirmed the words of the Law; it was she who told the magisterium what was what. There are those who suggest that Huldah herself wrote down the words of the Torah—I would love it if that were true, but it's unlikely for a myriad of reasons. We don't have anything else preserved about her life, about her words and actions, only this one moment. They could have taken the scroll to Jeremiah, Zephaniah, or Nahum, all of whom were likely available around that time, but they didn't. They took it to the Wise Woman Huldah. Her gender is entirely irrelevant to the writers, and their silence lends credibility to the story.

Now, there's strong evidence within and without the text that the Torah was compiled, written down, and heavily revised during and after the Exile, that moment of judgment Huldah was speaking of and that I've mentioned in other chapters. Historically, it wasn't so much found as a complete historical document as it was written to explain where the people of Israel came from and how they'd gotten to where they were. Every person was looking at their lives and saying, "How the hell did this happen?" and "Whose fault is this?" Scripture's answer is "Yours," and more broadly, "It was your selfishness as far back as creation itself, your unwillingness to do the hard work of caring for people not your own, and your inability to commit to Yahweh that brought this disaster." It's a harsh and painful message. Perhaps you can see why we don't always read it this way now—we don't want to hear it even 2,500 years later. Huldah, among the other prophets, was there to offer a sharp word of her own against the people's self-justification and to authenticate the word of God, which said the same.

There are so many more Wise Women—not only women who are wise but women who are recognized by the people around them as having gifts of foresight, of compassion, people who are called upon to offer their judgment and whom people listen to. They could be a neighbor or a CEO, the organist at your church or a best-selling author. The thing is, there aren't just Three Wise Women, just like there weren't Three Wise Men. The Three Wise Women (and Huldah, and your neighbor, and that TED talk speaker you love) were more than folksy ladies dispensing a helpful word here and there. They were revered, authoritative, even a little magical. They probably weren't paid for their work, and their gender precluded them from authority in official channels, yet who did Joab look for? Who did Saul look for? Who did Josiah look for? Who was it who spoke for the whole town of Abel? All four of these women exercised public power rather than private, their roles familiar to hearers of the time. They may not have had fancy robes of office as the magi are often depicted wearing, but they were listened to. Perhaps they had more freedom being adjacent to the system, not being beholden to the hierarchy. I was just in a meeting where we were asked to introduce ourselves not by our workplaces but by whom we are accountable to—perhaps these women, even Huldah, by virtue of their gender were accountable to the people, to those who sought them out, to God, rather than to whoever paid their salaries.

Who are we consulting now? What is it we're desperate about that drives us to seek out wisdom? I could rant a bit here about social media or celebrity pastors as inferior replacements for wisdom. I could say we rely on brain-altering substances like alcohol and caffeine and schadenfreude-induced dopamine to resolve our inner conflicts. I could complain that we long for reconciliation and redemption before we've done the hard work of justice. And perhaps all those things are true. We are desperate for meaning and stability and hope, and by God, we will take them anywhere we can find them, even if they're insubstantial. But I'd be willing to bet that you could name at least one Wise Woman in your life, whatever her gender, who speaks truth to you whether you like it or not and who you recognize as different and more and set apart. Their words and actions resonate with your soul as though you are the taut string on a piano being hit over and over by a hammer, vibrating with energy and sending music into the world.

My spiritual director is a Wise Woman. I've known her for fourteen years, among the longest relationships of my life. She has midwifed me through some overwhelming and difficult times, and I often don't really want to hear what she has to say. But I need it. Her wisdom is a gentle, curious, insistent finger plucking at my piano strings. I seek her out because I am desperate to be a better human. My massage therapist is a Wise Woman, though he is a man. He has helped my body release the pain and heartache it holds, has breathed in sync with me, has felt when I was laying down my burdens. I seek him out because I need to practice being here and now, being in my body and listening to its wisdom. Brené Brown is a Wise Woman, but you probably know that already. I've watched her TED talk on vulnerability easily a hundred times, and every time I hear something different—something that calls me out of myself, something that sees me uncomfortably clearly. I seek her out because I need to be reminded of who I am and who I could be.

Who are the Wise Women in your life? Seek them out. Ask them your hardest questions. Listen to them. Thank them because it's a thankless job to be wise, whether you're a magician or not.

12

Vashti and Esther

Fierce-Ass Women

Esther said, "A foe and enemy, this wicked Haman!"
—ESTHER 7:6

Vashti was Ahasuerus' queen, which meant she was queen over everything and nothing. Ahasuerus was king over everything you could see, from here to there, with "here" being wherever you the reader are right now and "there" being the farthest, most exotic locale you can imagine. All of it was his. (Scripture says India to Ethiopia, the 127 provinces between them, and the vast armies of Persia and Media—in other words, the whole world. This is the first hint in the first verses of the book that the story will be an extreme exaggeration. Anytime something in the Bible seems ridiculous, know that that's precisely the point.) Everyone who had a thought in their head knew he was king over everything. Therefore, Queen Vashti was queen over everything, from here to there. But she was a woman and had no real power, so she was also queen over nothing, from here to there.

Queen Vashti's husband held a banquet. For six months. Because what's the use of being king if you can't just party and golf and pose for photos and do what's right in your own eyes all the time? Everyone who was anyone was there. His officials, his ministers, the entire armies of Persia and Media and all their noble governors—hell, even the presidents of the school boards got invited. Ahasuerus provided food and wine and dancing and beautiful rooms and gardens and karaoke and poker tables for these folks for six whole months, all to display how much wealth and power and influence he had. Truly, Ahasuerus was full of his own grandeur.

At the end of this extreme party, when everyone was pulling on their coats and hats and the caterers were wearily cleaning up the plates and spilled food, he had another party, like you do. It was only for seven days, which might seem tame considering the one that came before, but this one received special attention. This time, Queen Vashti had her own party with the women, separate from the men, because as lovely as all the decorations at the king's weeklong party were (and scripture walks you through the palace pointing them all out, from the curtains to the cups), it was a drunken mess. They drank "without restraint," and King Ahasuerus actually ordered folks to "do everything they wanted to." Some scholars say this is a saturnalia, a sacred celebration originally to the god Saturn when everything is upside down, when all can speak their minds, and the foolishness of it is the point. Alternatively, the upside down–ness is what allows the plot to move forward—it's what the Jewish readers need to see: that the world of exile in Babylon they're living in can and will shift dramatically in their favor. But I'm getting ahead of myself.

On day seven, when the king was "merry with wine" (read: "drunk off his ass"), his guests suggested he should show them how beautiful his wife was by having her come in wearing her crown. Rabbis say what they meant was wearing *only* her crown, because why else would she refuse? Seems like a likely request considering the level of the party, but either way, she refused. Some rabbis say it's because of her modesty, and others say it's because she actually had leprosy or had grown a tail and was embarrassed. The text itself doesn't say anything, but boy did Ahasuerus. He was angry as only a drunk, self-obsessed king can be. *What a bitch*, he thought. *She probably teases every man she meets. She's probably uglier than I remember, anyway,* or some such justification. As was his custom, he consulted his advisors—all very upright, learned men, men you've heard of, really just great men, top-notch, believe me. He said, drunkenly, "I called her, and she won't come. There's got to be some sort of legal precedent. I can sue her or throw rocks at her, right?" One of these really great men said, equally drunkenly, "Yes, indeed, not only has the queen done terrible wrong to the king—deep and hurtful wrong—but her saying no to his tiny, inoffensive request has hurt the entire kingdom and every governor and mayor and city council member. We are all shocked and appalled by this behavior."

The king and his advisors didn't just get upset about Vashti; they were concerned about how Vashti's "contempt" would affect their own wives, and so they passed an unchangeable law exiling Vashti (or possibly executing her, according to some rabbis) from the presence of the king and reinstating the status quo that husbands were in charge of their own houses. I mean, obviously, one woman not doing what her husband asks in one situation means that all women everywhere will never listen to their husbands ever again. You get that, right? The narrator says, "Even now, this very day, noble ladies whisper the story to each other and rebel against every man." Can. You. Believe? Oh, and did I mention that the king also stipulates in the wording of this law that he will get himself another wife? To be fair, the book itself doesn't judge the process by which Ahasuerus chooses a new wife—he is a fool for most of the story, but the process itself is instituted without comment. It's just part of the plot.

(In a fascinating aside, rather than leave this story to be one about the foolishness of insecure men with the power of government behind them, some commentators have decided it's an allegory with Ahasuerus as God and Vashti as Evil personified. He is seen as righteousness itself, and she supposedly forced Jewish women to work naked on the Sabbath. Because of how capital *E* Evil Vashti is in this interpretation, she cannot come into God's/Ahasuerus' presence unclothed, for she will be exposed and there will be nothing there. I mean, I like "The Emperor Has No Clothes" as much as the next person, but that interpretation could also be a way to slough off blame or bad decision-making from the king.)

After all this mess, the king felt better, his anger dissipating along with his drunkenness, and he remembered Vashti and what he had done. Did he regret or mourn or sag in relief? He did nothing. But he did perk up when his advisers suggested a kind of "The Bachelor of Persia" scenario wherein they would get beautiful virgins from every province of the kingdom and have them dress up all pretty for him so he could pick a new queen.

It's here that we meet Esther and her cousin Mordecai. Esther's parents died when she was young, so Mordecai adopted her and raised her to be a good woman. (Some ancient rabbis interpreted "adoption" as marriage rather than a father-daughter relationship—again, I do take this possibility seriously, yet nothing else in the text suggests it.) The two of them were Jewish, which in the Hebrew scriptures you might think would go without saying, but here, they were a minority in Ahasuerus' realm, and their identity as Jews was pivotal to the exciting plot before us. Mordecai was known to be Jewish, but he asked Esther to keep her faith hidden for reasons we are not told, though we assume, given later plot points, that her ancestry would make her less desirable or even a threat.

Esther was famously beautiful. Think of little kids dressing up as princesses or the haunting *National Geographic* cover of the Afghan girl with piercing eyes (Sharbat Gula is her name—read her story sometime). She was so beautiful that when the king's reality television, wife-choosing flunkies came to town, she was swept up and taken to the harem. She didn't "look Jewish," and no one questioned her. She wasn't just a pretty face, though—she was quick-witted and perceptive. She was able to set herself up with the best food and sleeping area by making friends with Hegai, the eunuch in charge of the harem. She made other friends, I like to think, because she and the others were meant to have some sort of "cosmetic treatment" that turned out to last an entire year: six months doing something with myrrh and six months with perfumes and cosmetics. Sounds a bit like Bollywood doing *My Fair Lady*, which, come to think of it, would be awesome. Can we get someone on that?

After the year of milk baths and Botox and whatever else, each woman was sent up to the king to see if he would give her a rose—sorry, I meant, to see if he would make her queen. Each woman could take something with her when she went, and Esther showed great wisdom in asking her friend Hegai what to take. Scripture doesn't say what he suggested—Condoms? A very fine hat? A pasta spoon? Early rabbis wrote that, rather than an item, it was advice she took—advice to appear modest and not to partake of the cosmetic treatments because men like women to look natural and not all painted up. Since the story is so concerned with appearances and decorations, including her own later, this seems disingenuous. Whatever it was, in addition to her great beauty, it turned Ahasuerus' head, and she won the rose. Or the crown. And because he'd chosen a new queen, the king presided over yet another fabulous party. Why not?

While Esther was a part of the harem, her adoptive father Mordecai would stroll by their courtyard regularly to check on her. On one such stroll, he overheard two of the king's advisers angrily discussing how to kill the king. He told Esther, Esther told the king, and the men were hanged. And they all lived happily ever after—almost. First, we have to meet our mustache-twirling, scheme-making, genocide-planning villain, Haman.

In Jewish religious tradition, when the book of Esther is read aloud on Purim, you're supposed to yell and spin noisemakers to drown out Haman's name so no one can hear it spoken—he's that bad. He got promoted because of the two who were hanged, and he was damn full of himself, with people bowing and scraping in his presence because of his elevated self. But Mordecai did not bow down. Why would he? Haman was just a dude, not God, not even a king. And it turns out that their ancestors (Jews vs. Amalekites) had a feud that they were still participating in. For days, this went on: Haman would walk through the halls or around the streets, everyone would drop to their knees and stare at the ground, and Mordecai would stand off to the side and incline his head a little. Folk told Haman, who took the most logical and noble path: he decided to kill all the Jews in the whole kingdom, from here to there. I mean, obviously, a single Jewish man not doing what an authority figure asks in one situation means that all Jews everywhere will never listen to authority ever again. And therefore must all die. That is a bad, bad thing. You get that, right? (Lord, I hope you don't, in fact, get that.)

Haman went to the king and said, "Listen, my dude, there are some 'people' all spread out and hidden in your kingdom who aren't from here. They look different, and they're taking our jobs and they're raping our women and we have to do something about it. I can draft a law for you—one of those unbreakable laws you pass without thinking about it all the time, and we can 'deal with them,' ok? Oh, and here's a bunch of money. Not a bribe! Just, you know, a gift from a friend." And the king said, "Yup, fine, great, get it done." Were the Jews well-known? Were they hated by people besides Haman? The story doesn't say. The command went out to every part of the kingdom, from India to Ethiopia, that the authorities there should (1) destroy, (2) kill, and (3) annihilate every one of the Jews on the thirteenth of Adar, a year away, and also take all their stuff. The tone of this book is playful, and I'm joshing a bit with the phrasing here, which really is that ridiculous, but it's also important to note that Haman was very much neither the only nor the last person to hate the Jewish people for no good reason and seek their destruction. But don't worry—he, at least, will get his.

Mordecai somehow obtained proof of this plot, and like the assassination plot before, he told Esther. "You must go to your husband and beg for our lives," he said. "Me?" she asked. "When people show up to see him unannounced and un-asked-for, he just waves his hand and the guards kill them. Abba, I could die!" Mordecai said, "My dear, you'll die anyway because of this law—you're still a Jew. Being queen won't make a damn bit of difference." As exaggerated as the story is, this moment between the two of them is so real. I see them holding each other's arms or sitting close, staring unblinking into each other's eyes, father and daughter. Esther saw and knew she must put her life on the line to save others, and it was scary. Mordecai didn't want to ask this of her, but he said, "If you keep silence at a time such as this, help will come from another quarter." If you keep silent at a time such as this. At a time such as now, whenever you're reading this. What is the silence you keep? Who are the people who need your voice?

Mordecai asked, "Who knows? Maybe this is why you're the queen." In the only reference in the book to Jewish spiritual practice, Esther asked her people to fast for three days before she went to see the king. She took the fasting time to build a plan and work out how she could plead for her people. How could she get her husband to see her and take her seriously? She dressed up in her fanciest jewels and silks to look as queenly as possible. The Talmud says it was an inner fanciness and outer modesty and that the king was awed by her je ne sais quoi. It's possible, sure, but it seems a bit circuitous. She stood just outside the doorway in her finery and waited. She waited like a protestor going to their first march, knowing there's a distinct possibility they could be gassed or arrested. She waited with her heart pounding and her stomach in knots, jumping at every sound, certain that each moment she'd be dragged forward and put in chains. Ahasuerus saw her waiting and said, "Esther! Come in, come in! It's been a minute. My dear, how can I help you? Even up to half my kingdom." Was he serious? And can you imagine the relief? She began to enact her plan: she invited the king and Haman to dinner in her part of the palace. The king did love a party, so this was not a hard sell. At dinner, he again asked, "How can I help you—even up to half my kingdom." She demurred—was it part of the plan, or did she lose her nerve? It's hard to stand up to authority and to come out of the closet—and invited them to dinner again the next night.

There's this amazing and ironic interlude between the banquets where first Haman boasted ad nauseam to his friends and wife about how great he was and how deplorable Mordecai was. They suggested he have a gallows built and hang him, which he thought was a capital idea. In the meantime, the king had insomnia, asked for the records of recent legal cases so he could fall asleep while reading them, and discovered that it was Mordecai who was responsible for saving his life that one time, but did we even give him a fruit basket? No, we did not. And what a coincidence—when trusted advisor Haman came waltzing in to request Mordecai's hanging, pretty please, the king asked him how best to honor someone. Haman, full of himself as always, thought the king wanted to honor him, so he spun a ridiculous fantasy of public accolades and riding the king's horse, only to have the king clap his hands delightedly and say, "Yes, do that. You go get that horse and here's my robe and you be the one yelling for my friend Mordecai." How hilariously mortifying.

At Esther's second banquet, the king offered yet again, "I'll do whatever you like, up to half my kingdom." This time, she told him everything: that she and all her people were to be destroyed, killed, and annihilated. Ahasuerus said, "What? No way. Who did this terrible thing?" I mean, besides you, sir, for being a fool and letting your courtiers make dumb unbreakable laws in your name? But also, "He's in this very room. . . . It was Haman!" There's a bit when the king needed a moment to process all this and went out on the veranda for some air and Haman threw himself on Esther's mercy. One of the servants casually observed, "Say, there's a hastily erected gallows out here. Just saying." And the king had Haman hung on his own gallows. Delicious.

Esther pleaded with the king to have a new set of letters sent to keep the Jews from being slaughtered by his unbreakable law. He agreed, and the new version of the law reversed the ruling entirely, now allowing the Jews in the kingdom not only to defend themselves on the thirteenth of Adar but also to (1) destroy, (2) kill, and (3) annihilate any who would attack them—including all ten of Haman's sons. And they held another celebration in thanksgiving for being spared and for Esther for saving them, which they called Purim, after the Hebrew word *pur*, or "lot," because Haman threw lots to decide when to try to exterminate them. And *then* they all lived happily ever after.

Vashti and Esther are such remarkable women in such visible roles. Vashti's part is pivotal and meaty, though small, and Esther emerges as a true biblical hero, doing the fearful, necessary thing "at such a time as this." The book does not judge either of their sexual and marital choices; it is later commenters who get all aflutter. Esther doesn't have to be dowdy on the outside in order to have inner beauty and courage. Vashti doesn't have to be evil to have refused the king. Esther doesn't have to reject the whole patriarchal system to stand up to power. Vashti and Esther are not easy women to categorize, and I love them for it.

Reading these stories from a feminist perspective never requires having to read the women and their stories in only one light. The point of feminism is not to create a new set of require-ments women must adhere to in order to be acceptable but to allow women to choose their own paths, whether they are loud or demure, public or private, nurturing or contentious. Esther is as much a liberated woman wearing her fancy clothes and jewels and acting the decorous wife to save the whole of her people as Vashti is for refusing to show off her body to her husband's slavering bud-dies. There is no wrong way to be a woman, no wrong way to be a feminist—other than maybe by putting people who disagree with you into a box labeled "disgusting and objectively wrong" (*cough*, J. K. Rowling . . .).

The book itself isn't easy to categorize and doesn't apologize for being almost entirely areligious. For centuries, scholars and believers on the ground have struggled with why this book is included in the canon of scripture. And it very nearly wasn't. It has zero mention of God, of prayer, of religious practices, of law and covenant. There is one minuscule reference to fasting and that's it. There's a famous translation of the Hebrew Bible into Greek from the mid-third century BCE called the Septuagint. The trans-lators saw fit to add a ton of religious passages—including prayers, a vision, Esther as a clearly practicing Jew, and the name of God over fifty times—just to alleviate the discomfort folk felt. Where is God in this story? Right here, don't worry!

But those additions aren't in most modern Bibles because the story works on its own. Most of our lives are not obviously religious. God is absolutely present in and under and around everything that happens, but we're not constantly praying or sacrificing doves or singing "A Mighty Fortress Is Our God." Well, most of us, anyway. No, our religion is expressed at school boards or in making dinner or while marching in the street for justice. Maybe God's name is mentioned, maybe not, but God is present regardless, and we are still in touch with God even when they aren't mentioned. God was surely walking alongside Vashti and Esther and Mordecai and even Haman, though, bless him, Haman seemed to be entirely blind to it. This book is about a powerless member (a woman) of a powerless minority (the Jews) triumphing over evil. It's a tale of hope for a people living under oppression. Esther and Mordecai live out their call to justice and life, and isn't that exactly what God and the prophets are constantly calling us to?

Remember that movie *The Mummy* that came out in the nineties with Rachel Weisz and Brendan Fraser? There's a moment when the two teams of archaeologists-cum-grave-robbers are at the City of the Dead and the leader of one group says to one of the men with him, "They are led by a woman. What does a woman know?" This is precisely what generations of scholars, particularly Western Christian scholars, have said about Esther. Of course she needed advice from Hegai and Mordecai—how could she possibly have known what to do? How could she possibly be the hero? No, it's Mordecai who is the true hero of Esther—the righteous man, struggling to be heard. And poor Ahasuerus, under the weight of condescending or shrewish wives. This, too, is disingenuous and a refusal to read the text as it is. Mordecai is indeed a hero, but the book is about Esther, the one no one expected to lead, the underdog, even a little bit the trickster, who God chose (even if God isn't directly mentioned).

Maybe she won because she led with her gender expression—sweet dresses and home comforts and demure looks. Feminism isn't about every woman shaving her head and wearing sensible shoes and "acting mannish," whatever that means. It's about women having a choice, having agency, not being boxed into one way of doing things because of our genitals. And, to be clear, the same is true for our trans siblings—biology is not destiny. This means that a person who wants to wear sweet dresses and perfect the comforts of home and be demure is damn well just as valid as the forward, overbearing, and forceful ones of us. Neither is the only right way to be, and this story doesn't tell all women they should be like Esther. Except to say we should stand up.

The first protest I went to in the summer of 2020, just after the murders of Breonna Taylor and George Floyd, was peaceful—loud, to be sure, and angry and sad, but peaceful. Once the hundreds of marchers got to downtown Cincinnati, though, we were met with police in riot gear lining the streets ("Why are you in riot gear? We don't see a riot here."), and we were herded from behind and on the sides by dozens of police cars with lights flashing and every single siren blaring. It was an incontrovertible display of dominance and intimidation. We came with signs; they came with assault rifles. And they looked to me like little boys playing dress-up. They formed walls in front of City Hall, the courthouse, and, weirdly, the Catholic cathedral. But directly opposite that church, zero officers of any kind stood in front of the venerable and gorgeous synagogue. "What are you protecting here, friends?" I wanted to ask.

It felt to me that we were like Esther, fearful in the face of power, standing up against overbearing violence, not keeping silence at a time such as this. And it feels to me that we can channel Esther's spirit at any time, seeing the pain in the people around us and responding, whether it's asking if someone needs a tissue or a meal or refusing to dance to the tune of the fools in power. It's not easy to say no, but as I've said elsewhere, the way you are is not inevitable. The way *we* are is not inevitable. Esther and Vashti show us the way.

13

Judith

Antifa before It Was Cool

Her sandal ravished his eyes,
her beauty captivated his mind,
and the sword severed his neck!

—JUDITH 16:9

L ong ago and far away, there lived a fair maiden named Judith.
Well, she wasn't a maiden really, being a widow, with her beloved
husband dead for three years. But her skin was dewy and her eyes
sparkling. She was so beautiful, it made men and women weep
and stumble and drop whatever they were carrying. Everyone who
saw her remarked on her beauty and what it could mean. Everyone. Her loyal maid doesn't have any lines, and there's a eunuch
who doesn't seem to care much, but everyone else, individually
and corporately, was enamored to the point of ridiculousness at
how aesthetically pleasing Judith was. Beguiling, the Bible says in
English: enticing, tempting, seductive. A follow-up question, if I
may? Was she actively enticing people, or were people enticed by
her? Active or passive voice? The answer is yes. People projected
their desires on her, and she used what she had to get what she
herself desired.

In addition to her great beauty, Judith was also incredibly
wealthy. When her husband Manasseh died, he left her all he

143

had—livestock, property, servants, and fat stacks of cash. Even so, in her grief, she lived in a tent on the roof of their house, fasting and praying every day, wearing black and weeping. Her devotion to both her husband and to God was renowned in the city—her every action grew like a grapevine from this devotion.

So beautiful, so rich, so faithful: what a combination. You simply can't imagine anyone any better than Judith. She reminds me of my friend Chris: he's good at his job, square-jawed and handsome with a wide smile, a devoted husband and father, a ridiculously good cook, able to talk to literally anyone about literally anything, devoted to his faith, and just the nicest person ever. You almost want to hate him, he's so, so faultless, but you just can't on account of how nice he is. Chris is a modern Judith. With somewhat less beheading.

Before we learn all this, though, the writer of the book that bears Judith's name shares with us her pedigree, the genealogy tying her directly back to her great (×15) grandfather Jacob, son of Isaac. You might think, *Everyone has those genealogies in the Bible, and they're deeply boring*, and I'm delighted to tell you you're wrong. Not everyone is so fortunate to have a long, boring genealogy—definitely not women—and also, they're not boring. Ok, they are kind of boring if you don't know what you're looking for. Like, Jesus' genealogy in the Gospel of Matthew goes on for some time, but it includes four fascinating and awkward women: Tamar, who righteously seduced her father-in-law; Rahab, who hid Israelite spies from the police; Ruth, who went from refugee to grand dame with a roll in the hay; and Bathsheba, who was raped by a king and became the power behind the throne. Similarly, Judith's genealogy isn't just a dry list of names; it's a whole political document, and a mocking one at that. The names of her ancestors in this list are famous people from various eras of Israel's history (including superstar High Priest Hilkiah referenced in the Huldah chapter). One commentator says this genealogy was meant to mock people who invented fancy family histories because they were nobodies. The author was simultaneously building up Judith's authoritative pedigree and throwing shade at their contemporaries' vanity. That shit cracks me up.

Anyway, we meet Judith in the middle of a war zone. Her town of Bethulia had been under siege from Nebuchadnezzar's army, and the people were *thirsty*, y'all: for water, for food, for the emotional energy to deal with this mess. They're mad as hell, and they're not going to take it anymore! Relatable content. The elders of the town decided to put their trust in God, but only for the next five days. If at the end of that time God hadn't stepped in and done something, anything, they'd surrender. Judith, radiant in her mourning clothes, sent her maid to summon the town elders, who came immediately. She had pull in this town, even if she'd been living on her roof for three years.

Judith said to the town elders, "Y'all got it wrong. You can't give God an ultimatum. Who knows what God will do: maybe save us, maybe not—ain't up to you, though." She said, "In unrelated news, I've got my own plan." I am reporting her words here in abbreviated form for comedic effect—in actuality, Judith speaks more in this book than any other woman in scripture and more than most men. She castigated them for not trusting God, she prayed extensively, and she gave orders, clearly expecting them to be followed. She was well-reasoned and insightful. After her first speech, elder Uzziah said, "You are so right. We all know it. Our thoughts and prayers go out to the people, you know?" And Judith responded, "I mean, sure, I'll pray, but I'm going to do more than that. I've got a supersecret plan that'll fix everything."

When Judith prayed, unsurprisingly, it was beautiful and intense. She prayed thanksgivings for all the times God had helped the helpless, and she prayed that her plan would succeed: "Give to me, a widow, the strong hand to do what I plan" (Judith 9:9). In other words, God, wouldn't it be great if it were a woman who destroyed their arrogance and lies and brought justice? And what if it were me? It's so wild, it just might work. It seems like a fair request, only that's not how it usually works. Typically in scripture, human plans fail or are ridiculed by God, who is Wonderful

Counselor, Director of Planning, and Party Organizer. Here Judith has worked out her heist on her own, and—spoilers—it's gonna work.

Judith went home and prepared for her caper. Her maid packed a bag of delicious, kosher foods for their journey. Judith put on her most intoxicating perfume and eyeliner so sharp it could kill a man. She wore her most intricately woven gown, the cloth draped and stitched to set off her curves and the warm color of her skin. Her maid did her hair in a dramatic, tousled style, artfully reminiscent of the morning after. Think Sophia Loren cast as James Bond. The overall effect said "date night"—a dinner party with a suggestion of the bedroom. When she and her maid left the house, when she waved her hand commanding the elders to open the city gates, they and the whole town stood slack-jawed at her comeliness, her allure, her pulchritude. I'm telling you, every damn time.

Anyway, the two of them walked a little way from the city and—"My heavens, I didn't see you there. How surprising"— they were captured. Step one of the plan, check. She said to the enemy soldiers, "My people will lose this battle either way, so I thought I'd just pop over to old Holofernes and let him know a back way into the city. No big deal." Her beauty was blinding and therefore trustworthy, apparently, so they said, "Ok, cool." So beautiful and trustworthy, in fact, that they sent a hundred armed men with her the short distance to General Holofernes' tent. There was "great excitement" when she appeared in the camp (a euphemism for communal arousal, perhaps), and the Assyrians were so impressed by her looks that they revised their opinion of the Israelites. They said, "How could we hate them when they grow such sexy ladies? Even their men must be super sexy, which is bananas, but we can't let them seduce the world!" One wonders if these soldiers have ever seen a beautiful human before.

Enter Holofernes. He was the general of Nebuchadnezzar's army, as powerful and rich as Judith was beautiful. He and his inner circle also found her beauty immense and surprising. Holofernes said, "Those hill people you come from were rude, and I can't let that stand, but you—you're so ding dang beautiful, you'll be taken care of; don't worry your pretty little head." Condescending, but also helpful to Judith's plan.

Judith responded with another long speech, saying, "I'm going to tell you the truth, and I won't lie, ok? No lying here, no deception." She said, "Remember that guy Achior you kicked out because he said you couldn't defeat Israel if God was on their side? It's all true! But listen, they're thirsty over there. They're desperate. They're about to do something stupid that will make God abandon them. God sent me to help you, to raise you up." She said, "I'll go out into a field and pray every night, and God will tell me when they've sinned, and then you can go destroy them." It's that one lie wrapped up in truthful and beautiful packaging so that Holofernes would believe her immediately: "God sent me to help you." That direct object *you* is so attractive, so flattering, so deadly.

Holofernes was pleased by all this, obviously. Through the haze of her beauty and the victory being handed to him on a silver platter, he couldn't see the lie. So he accepted it at face value and, reminiscent of Ruth, he said, "Your God will be my God." Just a quick aside: Why would you choose to follow a God who abandons their chosen people in the midst of massive suffering for a single, small infraction? Just because that God is going to give you what you want? Yeah, I suppose that'll do it. Regardless, part two of the plan, check.

And so that night and for several nights afterward, Holofernes invited Judith to his tent for a banquet. She attended, but she and her maid ate the food they'd brought, not because it was Keto or low sodium but because they kept kosher and because it cleverly laid the groundwork for part three of her plan. Every night after midnight, she and her maid would leave the camp and pray in the field, supposedly listening for God snitching on the Israelites.

On the third night, in a stellar moment of self-justification, Holofernes said to himself, "She is so beautiful, she must expect me to try to sleep with her. If I don't, she'll laugh at all of us in

Assyria." It's the assumption so many men have, that the presence of a woman automatically means sex. It's the assumption so many straight people have about LGBTQ folk as well, that queer identities are solely about sensuality and not simply parts of a complex whole. Humans are more than our sex drives; we are so much more than other people assume about us.

Holofernes was already incredibly turned on when Judith arrived in his tent, more so when she reclined, as was the custom, by the banquet table on a soft pile of lambskins. You can imagine a sumptuous Renaissance painting of a reclining woman, can't you? He said to her and his gathered attendants at the banquet, "Let's get drunk!" And she replied, confirming his plan in his mind, "Sure! This is the greatest day of my life!" She was telling the truth: she was delighted that the time had come to make him bleed.

Holofernes got so drunk that night he passed out. How sexy is that? His attendants left them alone in the tent, assuming that seduction and her nightly prayers would follow eventually. The quiet was sudden after the raucous dinner, the fabric walls absorbing even the smallest sound. Judith knelt by Holofernes' head and stared at his slack face. She prayed, her hands open and spread, her heart pounding. And then she stood and took his sword in her hands. She prayed again, took a breath, and cut off his head with two strokes. Part three, check.

She matter-of-factly handed Holofernes' head to her maid, who put it in their food bag—the food bag that they'd always had with them and that had become steadily emptier. The two of them went out into the field and the soldiers let them—what reason did they have to stop them? And so the two of them walked back to Bethulia, adrenaline rushing, blood dripping.

The story wraps up with Holofernes' head decorating the city walls, the people of Bethulia marching out to battle, the Assyrians rather comically calling for their general only to find him missing his head, and the Israelites chasing the Assyrians, killing them all, and plundering their bodies. Like you do. It's heavily reminiscent of Deborah and Barak defeating Sisera's army and Jael's tent peg, intentionally so. In the end, Judith became famous. Three times she was blessed by men in charge and was given all of Holofernes' possessions as a reward for her bravery, making her even more wealthy than she was in the first place. She donated it all to the Temple in Jerusalem, of course, because she was as devout as she was rich and beautiful.

And there was peace for a time.

It's such a satisfying story—this woman, looked up to but unexpected as a hero, dispatched the people's greatest enemy in a neatly planned, cinematic caper, then returned home to live quietly as she had before, satisfied with her life. It's not without problems or ambiguities, but it's fun! The mustache-twirling villains get theirs, our heroes triumph, and we, the readers, have some hope for our own day. Perhaps one of us can be Judith and change the status quo.

It's satisfying enough that Judith has become the subject of countless paintings, sculptures, operas, plays, and political treatises. A version of her story is read every year at Hanukkah. For a woman who probably didn't exist at all, she really gets around. Oh, didn't I say? This whole story is made up. From her lovely but vague name ("praised" or "Jewess") to the indiscriminate mixing of different time periods, the book of Judith is deliberately a historical novel or an allegory. This doesn't make it lesser, of course, because fiction can often tell us more truth than facts can. Metaphors give us more than the literal meaning. Judith may have been intended as propaganda against one family of rulers in Israel, the Seleucids, or another, the Hasmoneans. It's not entirely clear when it was written or for whom, only that it was composed in Greek and not part of the Jewish canon of scripture. You might have noticed already that this story is in the Apocrypha, the section of miscellaneous readings you can find in the middle of some bibles.

But it doesn't matter much because Judith's courage and deception have spoken to generations of humans living under tyranny. Or perceived tyranny. Judith has been used as an allegory against all kinds of rulers, including Queen Elizabeth I and the pope—any pope, really. The desire to see abusive kings or prime ministers or even school board presidents get what's coming to them hasn't changed since Judith's time. You're likely thinking of someone even now who lords over others, who takes what they want, whose aim is to destroy those who look or act differently than they do. It might be a social destruction as much as a physical one. Perhaps, even if you're unlikely to dress up in your prom dress and cut off their head with a sword, you long for justice and reparation. I sure as hell do. I want Esther and Deborah and Jael and Miriam to come storming in and make it all better with two strokes of a sword. Racism, generational poverty, sex trafficking, empty-suit politicians who can't be bothered to do the hard work of governing—it would be so much simpler if cutting off someone's head could solve our problems. And yes, I do see the irony.

There's a theme in the art world called "The Power of Women," which sounds incredibly inspiring, doesn't it? Looks it, too, with women depicted riding men like horses or cutting off their heads or otherwise exerting power over them. Only it's ironic. Rather than communicating something about liberation or transformation or even something entirely unrelated to gender issues, it's mocking, like Judith's genealogy—"How hilarious to see a woman in control of a man, how ironic, and unrealistic, and a little bit titillating." It really hacks me off, to tell you the truth. The artists' intentions in visually empowering women in this way don't serve to demolish the gender hierarchy—they reinforce it. But they don't have to.

So many generations saw Judith's power as transitory or funny, but so much of scripture is about God choosing people their society didn't value. The operable words there are "God choosing." Maybe it is funny that God could choose someone young or short or gay or drunk or female, but it's also God's choice. And maybe, just maybe, God chose those folks for a reason. It's jumping ahead by a lot, but Paul says in 1 Corinthians 1:27–28, "God chose what is foolish in the world to shame the wise; God chose what is weak in the world to shame the strong; God chose what is low and despised in the world, things that are not, to reduce to nothing things that are." Judith saved her people, which is both indisputable and shocking.

The text of Judith wants her to be both the victim of violence and the master of it. She claims the space of one no one cares for while defined by her great wealth and beauty. She is but a simple woman, the text says: powerless and demure, yet capable of extreme and necessary violence. She exists as a metaphor for humility, justice, strength, and chastity, a foil for sin of all kinds, as well as the fierce hand of retribution. She's sexually provocative, but it's only a performance—or is it? She is not one thing or another because the text wants to have it both ways. But even though Judith herself is fictional and a tool for literary and political disputes, she represents real human women who are not one-dimensional, who are complex, contradictory, and autonomous. Judith is us.

We, too, can stand up to tyrants, whoever they are. We, too, can change the situation we find ourselves in. Maybe it's speaking up in a work meeting when your coworker interrupts you or disparages you yet again. Maybe it's demanding reallocation of police funds to community-based development to raise up our Black siblings. Heaven forbid we find ourselves in a position like Dietrich Bonhoeffer, who conspired to assassinate Adolf Hitler, or Judith of Bethulia, who killed Holofernes to save thousands. And yet when is the moment when we put an end to oppression of any kind? How far does the tyrant have to go before we stand up? And what will you do when it's time?

14

Foreign and Bleeding Women

Time to Pick My Heart Up off the Floor

> She had heard about Jesus, and came up behind him in the crowd and touched his cloak, for she said, "If I but touch his clothes, I will be made well."
>
> —MARK 5:27–28

Do you remember that movie *Leap of Faith* with Steve Martin playing a traveling faith healer scamming the locals with "miracles"? I remember it being hilarious and touching, but it was the nineties, so who knows. It's about an abusive form of theology that says if you have enough faith, God will heal you and that if you're not healed, it's because you aren't faithful enough—your continued suffering is on you. In the end—*spoilers*—Steve Martin's character learns a very important lesson about compassion and community, but more than that, I remember the film asking, "What does it really mean to have faith?" Like, on the ground, in practical terms, what is faith like and what does it do? (The Alice writing these words right now is horrified that this is where this chapter is going: I don't have a real answer to that—do you?)

Jesus says if you have faith the size of a mustard seed (read: ridiculously small), you can tell a tree to uproot itself and jump into the ocean. Have any of you tried that? I mean, we're also told not to test God, so. . . . I've talked with so many folks who have been praying as hard as Jesus did in the garden of Gethsemane that their wife or grandfather or child would get better, and they don't—does that mean they don't have enough faith? What if your spouse cheats on you, even though you'd trusted them with everything you have? What if a global pandemic hits alongside an intense pushback on systemic racism and the end of one of the most traumatic presidencies our country has experienced and you don't know if there will be much of a world for your kids to grow up in because of climate change and you're late on your book deadline—how does faith make things better?

There are two nameless women in the Gospels who make me think it's not entirely stupid to have faith in something better. One is known as the Syrophoenician Woman (or sometimes the Canaanite Woman) and the other the Hemorrhaging Woman or the Woman with the Flow of Blood. A filthy, heathen foreigner and a bloody mess—that's how we know them. But we also know them as faithful, and not in a sweet, decorous way. These women are desperate, argumentative, confident, and risky. They are not pastel, soft-focus, downcast-eyed prints to hang next to your blue-eyed, white Jesus. They are loud, clashing-color, abstract paintings that grab your attention and fill you with energy and hope. They're like Kandinsky or Ivey Hayes or even my husband's favorite, Miro. These women are challenging, and they are us.

Let's give them some real names, though—they deserve that much. I'll call the Syrophoenician Woman Ruhi, which means "soul" in ancient Arabic and "to thrive" in Sanskrit. And I'll call the Hemorrhaging Woman Talia, which means "gentle dew from heaven" in Hebrew.

Ruhi was not from Israel. She was from somewhere round about Tyre and Sidon, which meant she was a foreigner, a Canaan-ite, of the people of Jezebel, and we all know what she was like. Ruhi's daughter was sick. Her other children had taken ill at dif-ferent times and eventually got better because of herbs or teas she'd made and, when they'd had the money, because they could call for a doctor. This time was different. They'd done everything they could, there wasn't any more money for doctors, and she wasn't getting better. Ruhi's tears had all but dried up from sitting at her daughter's bedside late at night.

Ruhi may or may not have had a husband, but if she did, he didn't help her talk to the rabbi Jesus as would have been expected. Ruhi knew men had rules about whom they could talk to—not women, and definitely not women alone—but she'd heard about this Jesus man. He'd healed all kinds of people, even the servant of that soldier, the centurion, or was the man his lover? Either way, Jesus was helping folks who weren't his own people. People said he talked about a world where everybody could find peace. That sounded nice to Ruhi. Far-fetched, but nice. And she needed a little peace. Could it be possible? Could he heal her little girl?

And so she went out of her house, out into the square, out where people could see how her pain was ground into her face. She looked around at all the men arguing theology, some of them gesticulating wildly, and wondered which one was Jesus. One man was sitting on the edge of the well smiling fondly at the rest of them. He put his hands on his lower back and pressed in as he stretched. She looked at this man and knew. He seemed kinder but also more firm, like there was something he could see that gave him strength and purpose that the others couldn't imagine. She shook herself; what a flight of fancy while her little one was burning up at home. She took a breath, approached, and spoke: "Son of David, sir, my daughter is very sick. They say she has a demon. Will you help?" She hadn't realized she was shouting until the end, when her voice broke. She felt the tears of defeat well up again and her face burning in embarrassment. Her husband or father or brother should be the one helping, not this stranger, no matter how kind his eyes were. In one of the two versions of this story, she waited, but there was no answer. She looked up to find the other men around him staring at her in silence. A couple of them edged over to the rabbi, and she could hear them saying, "Dude, this lady's yelling at us. You want us to get rid of her?" In the other version, perhaps he couldn't ignore her because it says she'd collapsed at his feet. Jesus, healer and rabbi, breaker of traditions and chains, looked at this suffering woman and said to her, "I've come to feed the children of Israel. I can't throw that good food to the dogs."

Did he just call her a dog? Did he just imply that she was begging at a table, that she was poorly trained, that, at best, she was a cute lap dog who should know her place? He really did. And we'll come back to that in a moment, I promise. First, hear her response. Our Ruhi was undaunted. She was desperate, and she believed, perhaps foolishly, that there could be something else beyond this moment of pain. She was not acquainted with Israel's God, but I believe she'd felt God, seen God in her relationships—felt something bigger than just herself or her family. She looked Jesus in the eye, and she corrected him. She said, "Maybe I am a dog, but even dogs eat what falls to the floor from the table." She was saying, "I, too, am human and deserving of help and salvation. I'm suffering. Help me." And he did. Like Judah centuries before saying Tamar was more righteous than he, Jesus said, "You are brimming with faith like a cup running over with wine. Your daughter is healed."

Jesus, son of Mary and of God, when faced with this woman's pain, insulted her. There is a boatload of commentators who will say that calling Jesus' words an insult is childish or oversimplified, then fall over themselves to show that Jesus meant it as a test or banter—both of which also feel insulting. Others suggest Jesus was describing her in a neutral or even positive way because he was comparing her to a group of philosophers of the time called Cynics who rejected certain cultural expectations, and because of that, people referred to them as dogs. See, he's not insulting her—it's a compliment because of her boundary breaking! Still others say the Greek here is a diminutive, so he's not calling her a dog but a puppy—a cute pup you'd play with at home. These are both stretches. Dogs in this form are referred to throughout scripture, and not in a cute or philosophical way. And even if he is referring to her as a puppy, that, too, is condescending for a man who reaches out to heal people all the time with little to no resistance. Why would he resist healing this particular woman's daughter?

I love Jesus' delight in other people, his desire to engage their minds and hearts with their bodies. I also wonder if sometimes he was misread by the people reporting about him in the Gospels or if, in the moment, his responses came off as jerk moves. When people remembered these stories and wrote them down, did they sometimes make him more like themselves, grumpy and exclusionary, than he actually was? Or was he indeed the zealous prophet whose words turned people off as much as they invited in? I like to think if we could have seen their eyebrows during this exchange, we would know exactly what was going on. They're so expressive, eyebrows. But of course, Jesus of Nazareth wasn't a marshmallow. He flipped the tables in the Temple and drove people out with a whip. He cursed a fig tree to death because it wasn't fig season. We have to remember that while he was divine, he was also human.

So human that he could make mistakes? Be corrected? It certainly seems so to me, though I've been helpfully corrected on that point my entire adult life—by churchgoers, by seminary professors, by well-meaning students. Commentators balk at the idea of Jesus changing his mind, at God changing or repenting (though God does precisely that in Genesis just before the flood), at Jesus being able to be corrected. Yet Ruhi in all her outsider glory, by her persistence, reverses the situation. If that doesn't mean she changes Jesus' mind, I'll eat my hat.

In the midst of the 2020 antiracist protests, I decided to directly message all my BIPOC friends to check in. If Black lives matter, do they matter to me in my daily life? Most folks were as fine as could be expected and pleased to be checked in with. My friend Adeola was pleased but also more honest. She said, "I reached out to you to get our families together months ago, multiple times, and you didn't respond. That hurt my feelings." What a painful thing to hear. We talked about it a bit, I apologized, and we've gotten together for (distanced) family fun, but still, why hadn't I messaged her before? Because her life and needs weren't as important as those in my in-group, even if that group is just my family?

This separation is cultural and systemic, but it's also minuscule and personal—how do we treat people asking us for help? How do we treat our own friends when we're busy? As Jesus says just before this story, it's not what is on the outside of us that defiles; it's what is inside. And what's inside, you shit out. Jesus' swearing here is a topic for another book, but indeed, what is inside us—race prejudice, nationalism, unshakeable standards of gender expression, greed, *sin*—we shit out with our words and actions. All of us, apparently, even those who claim God as a parent.

Even though the interaction with the healer Jesus was, at the least, uncomfortable, our friend Ruhi was ecstatic that her daughter was healed. After months of illness and uncertainty and the hovering specter of death, her little girl was healthy again. Certainly, there was still plenty of suffering to pass around, but the relief made her feel like skipping home as she used to do as a little girl herself. He was insulting, it's true, and she felt diminished because of who she was, but she was used to that sort of thing. Healed! Perhaps she would cook an extra portion of lamb that night for dinner to celebrate or light the delicate oil lamps her mother had left her.

Talia, on the other hand, came to Jesus to ask for healing for herself. She'd been suffering from hemorrhages for twelve years, scripture tells us. We don't know precisely what that might mean, but most folks understand this to be a surprisingly common issue for people with uteruses: her period never stopped. It's called menorrhagia—one's period lasting longer than seven days— and five percent of people who menstruate experience it. She could have been bleeding nonstop or having regular periods that lasted longer than seven days, which isn't just an inconvenience—it's painful and exhausting and can be dangerous. If you look up "abnormally long period" on Google, you'll find all kinds of health conditions that might cause it, including hemophilia and cancer.

But twelve years? How was she still alive and functional at all? Two of the three gospel accounts of her story say that the doctors she'd seen had not helped and she was now penniless because of the cost. Even now, women (and trans people and Black people) still report not having their symptoms or questions being taken seriously by their doctors.

Scripture is unsurprisingly closed-mouthed about the specifics of Talia's condition—talking at any length about "women's problems" of any kind was unsavory and just gross. Why is it that both women's healthy and unhealthy bleeding is considered impure? To be sure, it's not a festival experience when we menstruate; it's just nature. Seems like it's the femaleness of it all that men find off-putting. Near the beginning of the coronavirus outbreak, someone on Twitter noticed that "pro-coronavirus Michigan protestors have focused their rage at the state's female governor, but in Ohio the rage is focused not on the male governor but on the female health director. What a funny coincidence." This was my tweet in response: "So funny. So coincidental. Who could possibly have foreseen it."

Talia, exhausted, in pain, impoverished, and socially outcast, came to this faith healer Jesus in desperation. Maybe this wild-eyed man who everyone said healed the sick could help. Maybe he wouldn't freak out and push her away or hit her like the others did because she was ritually unclean and could spread that uncleanness to him. *Even so*, she thought, *I shouldn't try to talk to him. I should just casually brush up against his clothing—perhaps that would be enough. What if it's not?* her brain responded. *What if you're still the same outcast, unclean, filthy woman you've always been? What if he feels; what if he knows? You might not survive it if his goons come after you.* Her heart said, *No, I have no other choice, no other options. Like the widow of Zarephath, I will do this and then die.* She stood behind him, gathering her courage, and then she bent down and so gently but with such purpose caressed the fringe on the edge of his cloak. In two of the three tellings of the story, she was immediately healed the moment she touched the fringe. A relief like the cool of air-conditioning after working in the hot sun washed over her. It was like she could feel her body knitting together the way it was meant to. What delight! What lightness! She hadn't truly thought it would work. She hadn't thought past the moment of the touch, and now she was free!

But when Jesus wondered aloud who touched him (and Peter looked around at the pressing crowds and said, "Lot of people around, man"), our Talia heard him, and her fear came crashing back. This man who was so obviously powerful, would he demand she pay him for the healing? Would he have her beaten or sent away again for contaminating him with her touch? Or is this another example of an incomplete and damaging translation? Perhaps she wasn't afraid but in awe—filled with wonder, gratitude, mystification, and fright all in one. This faith healer Jesus was more than she could have imagined; he reminded her of a lion in a book she'd read as a child.

One doorway into understanding a story is where it's placed in the larger narrative. All three times it's told, Talia's is an interruption in another healing story about a leader whose daughter was dead or dying and who Jesus resurrected. That placement suggests to me that resurrection isn't only literal but also emotional and social. Talia was raised from the dead of her misery and ostracization. She was given new life. And the way Jesus responded to her restored her humanity: when Jesus asked who touched him, it was not to chastise her or to test her like Ruhi but to call her "daughter" where before she'd only been called "woman." I like to think he wanted to look in her eyes and really see this person who was so desperate and so brave.

Jesus said her faith made her well. You could be forgiven for thinking that something magical happened, the way Mark and Luke tell it, because it seems to be the robe and her touching it that healed her. Matthew hastens to say it wasn't until Jesus spoke that she was healed, though that's not necessarily proof of nonmagical work. The church for centuries has struggled with how to talk about miracles and healing in a way that clearly separates it from magic, something only superstitious and ridiculous people believe in, while staffs turning into snakes or more than five thousand people being spontaneously fed from a tiny bit of food are definitely, for sure, without a doubt not magic because of *reasons*. I myself often talk about how my priestly hands aren't really magic, how asking for what you need or saying the thing isn't magic, and yet they kind of are. Unexplainable things happen at the Eucharist and between people when they're vulnerable. "Magic" isn't really about prestidigitation but about the awe we feel in the presence of things we can't entirely explain. In all three iterations of Talia's story, Jesus said "your faith" has done this. Not the robe, not his words, *her faith*. Something unexplainable has happened, and she and we and maybe even Jesus, who is so often excited to see new things happen, are in awe of it.

I heard mystic Richard Rohr recently say that maybe we could retire the word *faith* for a time in favor of something like *trust*, simply because none of us agree on what *faith* means. I hear so often from folks outside of the church that faith is "belief without proof," a naive trust in a person who doesn't exist, a blindness to real pain and real innovation in favor of a fairy tale that allows us to ignore our responsibility for the way things are. And there are a lot of folks inside the church who might use different words but essentially agree. As I've said before, scripture isn't naive to the ways of the world and neither is faith.

Talia was desperate—after twelve years of illness, poverty, and helplessness, who wouldn't be? Desperation could be a sign of faith or fuel for it. And though she was powerless, she still reached for healing: the crowds around Jesus had to have been difficult to navigate, especially since many of them knew her. They might have shied away from her innocent touch in walking by, but they might just as well have tried to intimidate her out of the crowd and back home. Talia didn't just happen upon Jesus; she worked hard to get close to him. Such spiritual and physical work is a sign of faith, and it might reveal faith to others. Ruhi strove with God like Jacob in the wilderness and Job at the city gate. Her faith was fighting back, and it showed that God would listen. The book of James says, "Show me your faith apart from your works, and I by my works will show you my faith" (2:18). What we *do* isn't everything, but it signifies what's within us. In other words, by looking at what we do, you can tell if what's inside us is love or shit.

I asked folks on Facebook what it meant to them in a practical way to have faith. One friend who had needed a stem cell transplant to stop their cancer said faith was their continual reaching out for healing in the years before their donor arrived. Another said it was feeling foolish for going back to church but showing up anyway. Another friend described faith as openness to something new and still another as the belief that something else is possible. Indescribable confidence, choosing something and sticking with it, taking risks, taking one more step forward. Faith is choosing to recognize our own worthiness—this one from someone who had been in an abusive relationship—that we are created by God in the image of God. Faith, it seems, is not only multifaceted like the gem of scripture; it is also exceptionally challenging. Not just to have it in the first place, but to enact it. Faith takes courage to rely on something other than our sense of powerlessness or temporariness. It is the spark of possibility, the light of trusting and depending on another. *¡Sí, se puede!*

This story is not a report—it's theology. This means that it's not about the historical accuracy of what Jesus said or did but about God's reaching out, against the resistance of the culture at the time, across national, religious, and sexual boundaries, to offer healing to people the normals wouldn't expect. Healing miracles are very much about sudden recoveries; feeding the multitudes is very much about what seems to be a magically replenishing loaf of bread, and these, in themselves, are very good. But they are also about overcoming firmly held prejudices and generational trauma, and that is even better. In other words, healing is more than the physical cure; it's the gift of possibility when there seems to be none. That's what God is up to.

Ruhi and Talia have been my heroes for most of my life. At my installation (it's what we call the worship service where a pastor is formally accepted into a job, not unlike changing a lightbulb), I asked a friend to preach on Ruhi's story. I didn't realize until I'd finished the first draft of this chapter that I'd already written about her in my first book *Fierce* alongside the Woman at the Well. She is, it seems, constantly in my mind and heart, asking me to see further, to speak boldly. Talia walks beside me whenever I'm feeling inadequate, which is all the damn time. How could I possibly be worthy of healing or acceptance? *Who do you think you are?* asks my brain, and Talia says, "You belong here." Because this is at the core of my being, this sense of being an outsider.

We moved a lot when I was young, so I was always the new kid. I was the weird kid too—imagine that. One of my coping mechanisms for feeling rejected was to wrap that sense of rejection around myself like a cloak, wearing it like ironic armor: "Yeah, I'm miserable because you don't want to be my friend, but I'm actually cooler because of it. I'm outside your system of rules, man." Ruhi and Talia help me hang up that cloak. Their faith doesn't just make them well; it makes me well.

My clergy colleague Alex describes Ruhi's conversation with Jesus this way: "Dog as I am, you seem like a dog person." No matter what our faith is like, no matter how able we are to see God with us, no matter how much the world or we ourselves might think of us as dogs, God reaches out their hand to us in love.

15

Lesser-Known Moms

How to Parent with Body, Heart, and Mind

As one whom his mother comforts, so I will comfort you.
—Isaiah 66:13 (ESV)

The Bible doesn't have a consistent sexual ethic. Lots of folks think the Bible says marriage is between one man and one woman, but that's patently untrue in so many instances. Lots of folks think the Bible clearly forbids homosexual relationships, but that is also patently untrue. Folks think sexual pleasure—and particularly a woman's pleasure—isn't important in scripture: false. Folks think the Bible says whatever the hell it is that they personally have hang-ups about. But it doesn't. Or, at least, it doesn't say it consistently.

And the Bible doesn't have a consistent motherhood ethic either. Again, lots of folks think there's a standard of biblical motherhood, that all women are meant to be mothers, that there are clear dos and don'ts within scripture and, consequently, in the two thousand years of Christian tradition, but there aren't. Moms come in all flavors and feel all kinds of ways about it. Any book or chapter that says "Here's how God wants you—and also all the other women you know—to be a mom" is, at best, shorthand for something much more complex and, at worst, lying and hurting people.

I didn't want to write this chapter. It's not because it's too upsetting or violent like the one in *Fierce* about Jerusalem, and it's not because I'm somehow against motherhood, as some internet trolls might suggest about feminists. I am a mom. My own mother is the world's greatest mom (fight me). Some of my best friends are moms. No, it's because biblical motherhood or Christian motherhood is just too nice. There are whole sections of bookstores devoted to soft-focus, pastel-covered books to give to moms or moms-to-be encouraging them to be mild and submissive and domestic and agreeable and industrious and pious and in control of all the things. There's a whole Christian-industrial complex developed around making women think that being a good wife and mother is their highest or even their only purpose—and that they're never enough. It's like the Christian version of the makeup industry: "Ladies, do you have skin? It's ugly—buy product."

Biblical motherhood as we often conceive of it in the twentieth and twenty-first centuries is also just too restrictive. It plays on a sort of gender determinism: because I have a uterus, that means I not only must conform to certain behaviors but also must be genetically predisposed to like it. I hasten to say that I know there are many women who do in fact like complementarianism—a theology wherein men and women and God are truly happiest when they all conform to societal gender roles. I love baking and sewing and gardening, and I imagine part of it is because I was born a woman and was offered those things by society and church, but I also enjoy fixing bits of my car when they break and talking politics over a glass of scotch. What do any of those things have to do with my genitals or my gender? Precious damn little. I'm grumpy about this because I and every woman I know is more than wife and mother—we are scientists and pastors, artists and builders, addicts and lovers.

And yet. While it's true the births of my children were painful and filthy and unpleasant all around, they have led me to a deeper love than I could have imagined before. Growing older with my spouse has been such a gift as we both become better humans and fall deeper in love. These things don't define me any more than my height or my dislike of enchiladas, but they are part of me, as they are for many of you reading this. If you are a wife, of course you want to be better at that. If you're a mother, of course you want to be better at that. Thank God there isn't only one path to get there.

So I'm going to tell you about a few mothers in the Bible—some you've heard of, some you haven't. I'm going to tell you about some mothers I know in real life and what they struggle with.

The first thing you should know is that there are very few examples in the Bible of anyone actually parenting. There are a shit ton of stories of miraculous and also run-of-the-mill pregnancies. There are even more shit tons of stories about people once they grew up, their behavior and devotion to God directly connected to their parents'. There is extensive advice about how mothers (and fathers, to a lesser extent) should raise their children but precious little about how people actually raised them. Proverbs is the typical go-to for biblical parenting, but it's not as fulsome a guide as you might hope. It is famously on Team Corporal Punishment because a good beating never hurt anyone, apparently. It does say not to beat children to death, so there's that, at least. And Proverbs says to teach them all the things you know, especially about God. It says to be wise and firm and generous, and I love these things, but also—how? In essence, the Bible never claims to be a child-rearing manual; it's more aspirational about parenting than prescriptive.

Of course there are many mothers in scripture demonstrating their techniques—well-known mothers whose names are on the marquee in lights, whose stories are just as epic and difficult as the men's, and mothers who are only barely mentioned, women who may not even have names who were working through their own tragedies. You may remember Mary and Joseph frantically searching for twelve-year-old Jesus all over the city of Jerusalem for three whole days. Or you might remember Jochebed, mother of Moses, hiding him in a basket in the river to save him from

Pharaoh (or maybe to give him a more merciful death than the soldiers might). And Abraham and Sarah dealt harshly with Hagar and Ishmael, and then Abraham almost killed little Isaac. Naomi tried to protect Ruth and Orpah by sending them back to their own people. Rebekah looked out for one of her sons but not the other. Rachel, as a metaphor for all of Israel, wailed in grief when her children were exiled and killed. Bathsheba used her power to make her son Solomon king.

Then there was Rufus' mom, who Paul says is like a mother to him too. She's in a long list of men and women who are all clearly apostles in Rome. There was Timothy's mother Eunice and grandmother Lois mentioned only once, in passing, in a book about exciting church administration but with the implication that they were the stable, caring people in Timothy's life who showed him God. And there were the nameless mothers in 2 Kings who, again in passing, made an agreement in the midst of a famine to kill and eat their only sons. There are a handful of stories in both the Hebrew and Christian scriptures about children being gravely ill and their moms desperately searching for a miracle.

Parenting, whether mothering or fathering, is so damn physical. I can remember in my actual skin the feeling of my father's hand stroking my back when I threw up as a kid. I remember the gut-deep terror of standing over my son's crib and hearing his not-fully-formed larynx make scraping sounds while he breathed. I revel in my kids' bodies pressed up next to mine as we watch YouTube on my laptop, even as they're massive, bony, kind of stinky preteens. Our bodies are more than vehicles for our thoughts and feelings; they are us and they are important. They're the reason God became flesh and dwelt among us.

Elizabeth's and Mary's stories front-load the Gospel of Luke with women's words and women's bodies. John and Jesus, a couple of guys of some importance, are introduced to us through their mothers, through the undeniably physical experience of pregnancy. Luke is not necessarily known for his celebration of women's stories and bodies, yet he frames his work with them.

Mary, mother of Jesus—famously young, even more famously virginal (though that's a theological repurposing of a mistranslation), somewhat less famously radical—spoke to an angel and sang a protest song in response. Her cousin Elizabeth was old and barren like Sarah and so many other women, but she and her husband were good folks—blameless in the sight of God, it says. Seems like an extreme term, *blameless*, but it likely means they did their best to follow the Law, and more than ticking checkboxes, they were kind. Even so, she was barren for a long, long time, a deep wound to her and Zechariah. When she had her own annunciation and pregnancy, no one was more surprised than she.

These two beatific women—one young, one old—met to support each other in their miraculous pregnancies and to commiserate about their aches and pains and fears. Because motherhood is a fearful thing. Until only a couple hundred years ago, it was likely that mother or child or both would die in childbirth. Children can get sick and die at any time, especially before vaccines and antibiotics. Would they know what to do then? Would they be able to keep food on the table or bullies away? Would the occupying Romans be chill for just a minute so they could raise their children in relative peace? Mary seemed to sense the greatness and the precariousness of her son. And once John was born, the people who gathered around Elizabeth's house murmured to each other, "What then will this child become?" (Luke 1:66).

This story of two moms dealing with normal mom things is also a story about apocalypse. Every damn thing will change with the birth of Mary's son Jesus—new life, new fears, new possibilities are revealed. Elizabeth felt her baby move in her belly the moment she saw Mary, and she laughed and shouted, "Oh! It's you who carry the Son of God! How delicious!" This is the first time in Luke someone names Jesus as Messiah and the only one from a woman. While my own daughter is not the Messiah—I know, you're surprised—the moment I first felt her move, I was driving and I almost wrecked from the shock and the sudden tears of connection. There was this weird moment that had one foot in sentimentality and one in body horror when I thought, *There's someone in there*. I could feel her hard heel or elbow pressing outward like a tap on the glass. Something entirely new and also old as dirt was happening. Elizabeth and Mary in that same moment spoke prophecy, and their round bellies spoke of the new world that was coming and that is still coming into being right now. In the immortal words of Beck, "Things are gonna change, I can feel it."

In three of the four Gospels, another story explains that some of the disciples got real petty about who was going to be in charge in the kingdom of heaven. In two tellings, they're identified as the sons of Zebedee, literally "Sons of Thunder," begging the question of whether that's dad's name or their nickname because they were huge and loud. In one of those tellings, it was not the men themselves who asked but their mom. I resonate with this story so much, though mom is only mentioned the once. She'd been around Jesus long enough—perhaps one of the "certain women" who supported Jesus' ministry and who would have been called his disciple if patriarchy hadn't been a thing—and she was invested in his message. She said, "Listen, Rabbi, this kingdom you keep talking about sounds swell and you're going to need some help running it, yeah? My boys should be the ones you pick—sure, they're big and loud, but they're good boys, and they can keep things orderly, you know?" I can see her heart in this moment. She was not being petty; she saw how dangerous the world was, and she was looking out for them. She was saying to Jesus, "You'll take care of them when I'm gone, won't you?"

My husband and I have talked about how we are, as parents, working on planned obsolescence. The goal is for our kids to eventually not need us, hence teaching them how to shower and how to cook and how to admit when they're wrong and how to stand up for themselves and others. When I let myself think about how there will be a time I won't be around to watch out for them, a hole opens up in my guts and I weep. Right now as I write this, it's happening. This is part of being a mother: knowing that it will end. I wrote in *Fierce* about Eve's grief—not only that Abel was dead but that she couldn't stop it. That death moved into the neighborhood, and her darling children, even Cain, would suffer. Who will care for them when we're gone? So we teach them the best we can to live openheartedly, to be curious, to take out the trash.

In Acts, there's yet another Mary, mother of John Mark, who seems to have been part of the Christian resistance movement. The early church struggled for a few centuries with persecution—believers were accused of cannibalism and atheism, arrested, and sent to be tortured in public as entertainment. The apostle Peter had been imprisoned because of the persecution under King Herod. When he was mysteriously liberated from his prison cell, Peter ran directly to Mary's house to hide. This Mary was a bit like Mrs. Zebedee and Joanna and Mary Magdalene: she had enough money to employ a maid and seems to have owned her own house. Did she lead the church that met there in secret? Was she a protective mother figure? Did she have authority within their community, debating theology around the table with the others? Like Eunice and Lois and so many other mothers, we can only imagine. This Mary offers me courage like Corrie ten Boom or Rahul Dubey, who opened his home to over seventy antiracism protesters in Washington, DC, who were being beaten by police. This Mary asks me, "Who do you count as your children?"

What is it we need from moms in the existential sense? What are they for? The world around us—and our own church sometimes—tells us we're supposed to do all the things, to do them all well, and to like doing them. Trying to meet that expectation is exhausting. All I can say is that we're meant to do the best we can with what we have: moms, dads, childless folk, everyone. "What we can" might not be much on any given day, and "what we have" might be even less. I appreciate the widow of Zarephath, another biblical mom, saying to Elijah, "Look, dude, all I've got for me and my son is enough for a couple of biscuits that we're going to eat, and then we'll die. I can't cook for you too." The point of that story is something else entirely, but I hear her honesty loud and clear: this is what I have right now, and I will not pretend otherwise. The moms in the Bible do not call us to be the best ever, or to be blameless, or to say yes to whatever other people need.

People have given birth in all manner of desperate situations—along the trail of the Armenian Genocide and refugee paths out of Syria, in concentration camps and in extreme poverty—and they've fallen in love with their babies with the same ferocity we do when safe. My husband immediately loved our daughter at first sight, scrunched-up, old-man face covered in mucus and poop as she was. I didn't feel it until hours later when I looked at her sleeping face in dawning wonder. Some struggle to find that love or any sort of connectedness or blessing in having a child: people in captivity, people whose parents were shit to them, people who didn't intend to have children but now do, people who were raped. Motherhood and parenthood aren't one size fits all; they're a hot mess, even when you're excited about the prospect.

Unfortunately, it seems that loving your child from birth isn't a foregone conclusion. Years ago, I helped out a little at a local women's addiction recovery center where the children stayed with their moms instead of other family or foster parents. The moms took classes on interview skills and cooking, but one class they offered broke my heart when I heard the title: "How to Bond with Your Children." Some women—because of the depth of their addiction, or the generational trauma of poverty, or any number of other reasons—not only don't love their kids; they just can't conceive of how to go about it. This class seems like it might be the most important thing for all of us. To learn to touch another person gently, to practice curious listening, and to be vulnerable about how we feel and what we don't know? It's horrific to see and be seen like that. And we can't live without it.

There is something sacred about mothers, something holy. Oh, God, now I sound like those pastel-colored books in the Christian Inspiration section of the bookstore. What I mean is, mothers are literally necessary for the continuation of the human race, and uteruses are magical things to be able to make another person. We can all agree on that, right? It's literal new life that you can watch happen, like bread becoming toast. But there's something beyond even that magic. The Bible says mothers are sneaky, grief-filled, resigned, joyful, vulnerable, and enlightening. It says they're supposed to be patient and thrifty and meek but also ferocious and sexy, and honestly, I'm just done with "supposed to." If there's anything moms are supposed to do, it's show up. Show up to your soccer games or your violin recital, show up when you're a sobbing wreck and when you're walking on air, show up when you come out of the closet and when you need help organizing it. Show up when you're being a jerk to call you on it and then show up to help you navigate what that means. And that, friends—having someone show up for you physically and emotionally, even if they can't muster up a lot of energy—that is holy. That is magic. That is a gift, and it's not reserved for your literal moms—it's for all of us to give.

Acknowledgments

I was supposed to start this book in late 2019, and I didn't really write in earnest until the COVID-19 times were well underway. So I want to say thank you to those who are reading this now for making it through all this with me. It doesn't matter if we know each other—you're partially responsible for this book being finished simply by your existing. I mean, editor Lisa and husband Leighton and kids Abi and Jackson and also Professor Erica Massey and Rabbi Yitzi and his wife Dina as well as friend Annie were also helpful. But you, you were the one who kept me going. Thank you.

Appendix A

The Biblical Stories Themselves and Where to Find Them

Maybe you'd like to read the stories for yourself and come to your own conclusions. Please, be my guest. Here is a list of references for the stories you just read.

God Is Not a Man

God's womb, God as rock that gives birth. Job 38; Genesis 49:25; Deuteronomy 32:18

Mother bird. Deuteronomy 32:10–11; Ruth 2:12; Psalm 17:8; 36:7; 57:1; 61:4; Psalm 91:4; Matthew 23:37; Luke 13:34

Mother bear. Hosea 13:8

Human mother. Numbers 11:12; Isaiah 42:14; Isaiah 46:3–4; Isaiah 66:13; Isaiah 49:15; Psalm 131; Psalm 22:9; Romans 8:22; 1 Peter 2:2–3; Psalm 110:3; Deuteronomy 32:18; Job 38:28–29

Woman searching for coin. Luke 15:8

A mistress. Psalm 123:2

Female servant or wife. John 13:4–5

Image of God. Genesis 1:26–27

Midwife. Psalm 22:9–11; 71:6; Isaiah 66:9

Baker. Matthew 13:33

Breath. Genesis 1; Psalm 104:29; John 3:8

Wisdom. Proverbs 8:22–31; Wisdom of Solomon 7:22–8:1

Jesus as Wisdom of God. 1 Corinthians 1:24; Colossians 1:15–16

Sarah. Genesis 11–23

Rachel and Leah (and Bilhah and Zilpah). Genesis 29–35

Miriam. Exodus 2:1–10; Exodus 15:20–21; Numbers 12; Numbers 20:1–2

Delilah. Judges 16

The Levite's Concubine. Judges 19–21

Hannah. 1 Samuel 1–2

Michal and Jonathan

Michal. 1 Samuel 14:49; 18–19; 25:44; 2 Samuel 3; 6; 1 Chronicles 15

Jonathan. 1 Samuel 13–14; 20; 23; 31; 2 Samuel 1

The Queen of Sheba. 1 Kings 10:1–13; 2 Chronicles 9:1–12

Jezebel. 1 Kings 16–21; 2 Kings 9; 2 Kings 10

Huldah and the Three Wise Women

Medium of Endor. 1 Samuel 28

Wise Woman of Tekoa. 2 Samuel 13; 14:1–24

Wise Woman of Abel. 2 Samuel 20

Huldah. 2 Kings 22:14; 2 Chronicles 34:22

Vashti and Esther. Esther

Judith. Judith

Foreign and Bleeding Women

Ruhi. Matthew 15:21–28; Mark 7:25–30

Talia. Matthew 9:20–22; Mark 5:25–34; Luke 8:43–48

Lesser-Known Moms

Parenting advice, not necessarily recommended. Proverbs 13:24; 22:15; 23:13; 29:15; among others

Elizabeth. Luke 1:5–25; 1:39–80

Eunice and Lois. Acts 16:1; 2 Timothy 1:5

A mother forgets her labor pains. John 16:21

Mary. Acts 12:12–13

Mom of James and John Zebedee. Matthew 20:20–28; 27:56

Peter's mother-in-law. Matthew 8:14; Mark 1:30; Luke 4:38

Moms killing and eating. 2 Kings 6:24–33

Rufus' mom. Romans 16:13

Appendix B

Homework (a.k.a. Ideas for Further Reading)

You say you want to delve deeper into this surprising world of biblical women? Well, I'm definitely not the first to write about them, nor the last. There's a lot of crap out there, though, so here are a few suggestions to get you started.

Crenshaw, Kimberlé. "Demarginalizing the Intersection of Race and Sex: A Black Feminist Critique of Antidiscrimination Doctrine, Feminist Theory and Antiracist Politics." University of Chicago Legal Forum, 1989. Accessed February 8, 2021. https://philpapers.org/archive/CREDTI.pdf.

> The seminal work on intersectionality and how privilege and lack of privilege compound themselves. Important reading to better understand womanhood, race, class, and how they overlap.

Evans, Rachel Held. *A Year of Biblical Womanhood: How a Liberated Woman Found Herself Sitting on Her Roof, Covering Her Head, and Calling Her Husband "Master."* Nashville, TN: Thomas Nelson, 2012.

> Rachel's one-year journey of enacting everything the Bible says about how to be a woman. Insightful, lovely, and challenging—particularly the parts about *eschet cayil*.

Fiorenza, Elisabeth Schüssler. *In Memory of Her: A Feminist Theological Reconstruction of Christian Origins*. New York: Crossroad, 1983.

A classic of feminist biblical interpretation.

Gaffney, Wilda. *Womanist Midrash: A Reintroduction to the Women of the Torah and the Throne*. Louisville, KY: Westminster John Knox, 2017.

A scholarly and exhaustive yet incredibly approachable study of a ton of fascinating women by a fascinating woman.

Gentileschi, Artemisia. Her paintings. Yes, all of them. You're welcome.

She was more than a woman painter in an era when that was not allowed—she was a brilliant painter. Full stop. She famously painted the face of her own rapist as Holofernes.

Gill, Laverne McCain. *Vashti's Victory and Other Biblical Women Resisting Injustice*. Cleveland: Pilgrim Press, 2003.

A phenomenal book on a handful of biblical women and their counterparts today.

Greene, Mark. "Touch Isolation: How Homophobia Has Robbed All Men of Touch." Medium, August 7, 2017. https://tinyurl.com/d7n6yryz.

A beautiful and heartbreaking essay on modern "masculinity" and everyone's need for tenderness and touch.

Hadewijch. *Hadewijch: The Complete Works*. Translated by Mother Columba Hart. Classics of Western Spirituality. Mahwah, NJ: Paulist, 1980.

Medieval Dutch love poetry between a woman mystic and God, who is very much a woman. One of my personal favorites.

Harris-Perry, Melissa V. *Sister Citizen: Shame, Stereotypes, and Black Women in America.* New Haven, CT: Yale University Press, 2011.

Contemporary writing on Black women's inherently political lives and specifically the racist history of calling them Jezebel.

Ladinsky, Daniel, trans. *Love Poems from God: Twelve Sacred Voices from the East and West.* New York: Penguin, 2002.

Does what it says on the tin. A ton of poetic mysticism whimsically translated. You'll laugh, you'll cry—it's better than *Cats.* Though most things are.

Mirsky, Yehudah. "Feminine Images of God." Jewish Women's Archive. Accessed February 8, 2021. https://tinyurl.com/ehr3r93x.

An excellent brief article. Also recommended: the entire Jewish Women's Archive. Wander around and see what catches your eye.

Newsom, Carol A., and Sharon H. Ringe, eds. *Women's Bible Commentary.* Louisville, KY: Westminster John Knox, 1998.

Scholarly essays on each book of the Bible with particular attention to female characters.

Ruttenberg, Rabbi Danya (@TheRaDR). "I so adore Judith." Twitter, November 27, 2018. https://tinyurl.com/khr46tsz.

A hilarious and insightful thread on Judith.

Spiegel, Celina. *Out of the Garden: Women Writers on the Bible.* New York: Ballantine, 2012.

A series of essays and storytelling from a variety of authors exploring biblical women's stories.

Trible, Phyllis. *Texts of Terror: Literary-Feminist Readings of Biblical Narratives.* Philadelphia: Fortress, 1984.

Another classic, this one confronting some of the most violent and painful stories in our Bible. Trible is unrelenting in her exploration.

Weems, Renita. *Just a Sister Away: Understanding the Timeless Connection between Women of Today and Women in the Bible.* New York: Warner, 1988.

Womanist theology and storytelling.

Williams, Delores S. *Sisters in the Wilderness: The Challenge of Womanist God-Talk.* Maryknoll, NY: Orbis, 1993.

Reading the Bible from a Black woman's perspective.

Winner, Lauren F. *Wearing God: Clothing, Laughter, Fire, and Other Overlooked Ways of Meeting God.* New York: HarperOne, 2015.

Essays on all kinds of imagery for God that is not masculine, much of it having nothing to do with gender at all.

Websites to Explore

The Bible Project. https://bibleproject.com.

Charming hand-drawn animations for each book of the Bible exploring what's in them, their history, and basic theology.

Chabad. https://www.chabad.org/—in particular, their search function.

Use this site to look up women from the Hebrew Bible from a conservative Jewish perspective.

Farrell, Heather. *Women in the Scriptures* (blog). https://www .womeninthescriptures.com.

Similar to chabad.org, this is an interesting resource where you can read a little bit about a lot of women in the Bible from a Mormon perspective.

The Junia Project. https://juniaproject.com.

A fantastic and wide-ranging website advocating for the full inclusion of women in ministry and for mutuality in marriage.

A Couple of Thoughts That Might Be More Meta but Helpful, Nonetheless

Sprinkle, Preston. "What the Bleep Does the Bible Say about Profanity?" *Relevant*, August 22, 2014. https://tinyurl.com/dt47ucrn.

Why swearing is not only ok but helpful, particularly when talking about faith life.

Zierman, Addie. "Recovering from Legalism." YMI, June 29, 2016. https://tinyurl.com/ytx6766a.

A blog post about learning to read scripture through a different lens.

Notes

Introduction

xiii **"A trans man"**: Some of Peterson Toscano's work can be found here: https://petersontoscano.com/portfolio/transfigurations. He and others remark on the Hebrew phrase ketonet passim which means something like "super-fancy coat or dress." It's used only twice in scripture: for Joseph's garment and for the clothing King David's daughter Tamar wore in 2 Sam 13:18, described specifically as what virginal princesses wore. Please enjoy this phenomenal poem by J Mase III leaning into Joseph as trans: https://tinyurl.com/3uskm2h6.

Chapter 1

2 **"The only sex organ God has in the Bible is a uterus"**: See page 291 of Dr. Wilda Gafney's stellar book *Womanist Midrash: A Reintroduction to the Women of the Torah and the Throne* and the rest of it as well. She's brilliant.

4 **"Julian of Norwich wrote in the late 1300s"**: Julian of Norwich, *Showings* (Mahwah, NJ: Paulist, 1978).

4 **"And Anselm, archbishop of Canterbury, wrote in 1072":** Anselm of Aosta, *Prayers and Meditations of St. Anselm with the Proslogion*, trans. Benidicta Ward (London: Penguin, 1973).

Chapter 4

39 **"Miriam sang, and she was called a prophet. And later, when they wrote it down, her words were given to Moses":** Wilda C. Gafney, *Womanist Midrash: A Reintroduction to the Women of the Torah and the Throne* (Louisville, KY: Westminster John Knox, 2017), 98.

Chapter 10

115 **"This writer, often called the Deuteronomistic Historian, believes in 'military punishment for religious faithlessness,' according to one scholar":** Claudia V. Camp in *The Women's Bible Commentary*, ed. Carol A. Newsom and Sharon H. Ringe (Louisville, KY: Westminster John Knox, 1998), 102.

115 **"It doesn't just disappear because slavery 'ends'":** Read the Thirteenth Amendment to the United States Constitution, and you'll see why that's in scare quotes.

Chapter 12

135 **"Bollywood doing *My Fair Lady*. . . . Can we get someone on that?":** Guess what? We already had someone on that. *Man Pasand* came out in 1980 in India.

Chapter 14

156 **"Dogs in this form are referred to throughout scripture, and not in a cute or philosophical way":** Check out a selection of references to dogs here: Exodus 22:31; 1 Samuel 17:43; 2 Samuel 16:9; Psalm 22:16; Proverbs 26:11.

159 **"Someone on Twitter noticed":** That someone was @JHagner on May 3, 2020.

10/28